Diabetic Cookbook for the Newly Diagnosed

2000 Easy & Delicious Recipes to control Blood Sugar without Sacrificing Taste and to manage Prediabetes and Type 2 Diabetes. 60-day Meal Plan Included.

Lisa Mckeith

TABLE OF CONTENTS

INTRODUCTION

Diabetes is a chronic condition characterized by high levels of sugar (glucose) in the blood. People with diabetes have difficulty regulating their blood glucose levels and this can lead to a variety of health problems, if left uncontrolled. An important aspect of diabetes management is nutrition, because what we eat can greatly affect our blood glucose levels. Diabetic recipes are specially designed to be low in sugar, carbohydrates, and fat, while still being flavorful and nutritious.

In this lecture, you will explore the benefits of diabetic recipes and provide some tips for incorporating them into your diet.

Benefits of Diabetic Recipes

1. **Better Blood Glucose Control**: One of the main benefits of diabetic recipes is that they can help people with diabetes control their blood glucose levels. Diabetic recipes are typically low in carbohydrates, which can cause blood glucose levels to spike. By reducing carbohydrate intake, people with diabetes can better manage their blood glucose levels.

2. **Improved Heart Health**: Diabetes is a risk factor for heart disease, so it is important for people with diabetes to prioritize heart-healthy eating. Diabetic recipes often incorporate heart-healthy ingredients such as whole grains, lean proteins, and healthy fats. By following a diabetic diet, people with diabetes can reduce their risk of heart disease.

3. **Weight Management**: Maintaining a healthy weight is important for managing diabetes. Diabetic recipes are often lower in calories than traditional recipes, making them a great option for people looking to lose weight or maintain a healthy weight.

4. **Increased Nutrient Intake**: Diabetic recipes often incorporate nutrient-dense ingredients such as vegetables, fruits, and whole grains. By eating a diet rich in these foods, people with diabetes can improve their overall nutrient intake and reduce their risk of nutrient deficiencies.

Tips for Incorporating Diabetic Recipes into Your Diet

1. **Experiment with New Ingredients**: Diabetic recipes often incorporate ingredients that may be new to you, such as quinoa, chia seeds, or almond flour. Don't be afraid to try new things - you may be surprised by how delicious and satisfying these ingredients can be.

2. **Plan Ahead**: Planning your meals ahead of time can help ensure that you have healthy, diabetes-friendly options available. Watch out for cooking and freezing meals for later use, or prepping ingredients ahead of time to save time during the week.

3. **Focus on Whole Foods**: When planning your meals, focus on incorporating whole, unprocessed foods as much as possible. This can help ensure that you are getting a variety of nutrients and can help you avoid added sugars and unhealthy fats.

4. **Be Mindful of Portion Sizes**: Even healthy foods can be high in calories if consumed in large quantities. Be mindful of portion sizes when preparing and serving meals, and consider using smaller plates and bowls to help control portion sizes.

Types of diabetes

All types of diabetes have one thing in common: the presence of hyperglycemia. The most frequent is type 2 diabetes, but type 1 diabetes and gestational diabetes should not be overlooked, although they are less frequent forms of diabetes.

Type 1 diabetes

Type 1 diabetes mellitus occurs when the pancreas does not produce insulin. Generally, in half of the cases, it occurs at a young age (<25 years approx) with an incidence of approx. 3% of the world population. It is an autoimmune disease, therefore our immune system destroys the cells used for the production of insulin (ß cells of the pancreas), the main causes that contribute to the development of type 1 diabetes are:

- an underlying genetic predisposition particularly in ethnic groups more at risk (eg. Sandinavians and Sardinians)
- an immunological stimulus, often due to the environment in which one lives
- viral infections (including rubella,cytomegalovirus, coxsackievirus, retrovirus, and Epstein-Barr) which can infect and destroy pancreatic ß-cells
- an inadequate diet especially in children such as early exposure (<4 months) to gluten.

This pathology is irreversible, so the person with type 1 diabetes will have to take the necessary insulin from the outside.

Type 2 diabetes

The characteristic of type 2 diabetes mellitus, a metabolic disease, is high blood sugar, which represents about 90% of cases of diabetes. The pancreas does not produce a sufficient amount of insulin, or the insulin produced does not act correctly, our body is not able to use it in particular at the peripheral tissue level (insulin resistance). In general, type 2 diabetes occurs after the age of 30-40 and becomes more frequent with increasing age, especially in the presence of certain risk factors including:

- overweight (visceral/abdominal fat)
- lack of exercise
- unhealthy lifestyle habits (eg: diet rich in sugars and saturated fats, physical inactivity, alcohol)
- heredity (genetic predisposition)
- belonging to a specific race (Hispanic, Asian and American Indian in particular)

The pathogenesis is not entirely clear even if hyperglycemia develops when the production of insulin is no longer able to compensate for insulin resistance, consequently the liver "improperly" releases glucose into the blood, generating a situation of hyperglycemia. In the first phase, the body reacts to insulin resistance by producing a greater quantity of insulin, subsequently the production of insulin is no longer sufficient, laying the foundations for the onset of type 2 diabetes.

Other mechanisms associated with Type 2 diabetes that contribute to the onset of insulin resistance are:

- low levels of hormones (testosterone, estrogen, etc) which increase insulin sensitivity

- high levels of hormones (glucocorticoids, glycagon, adrenaline, mineralocorticoids, etc.) which increase insulin resistance
- water retention
- poor regulation of metabolism by the central nervous system

Moreover, insulin resistance can generate feedback mechanisms in the body that inhibit the production of insulin by the ß cells of the pancreas.

Gestational diabetes

It is a temporary condition, which generally occurs during the second half of pregnancy, when the woman's insulin is less effective. It tends to resolve soon after delivery, although women with gestational diabetes (read the full article here) develop a higher probability of becoming diabetic in the years following delivery, particularly in the presence of risk factors.

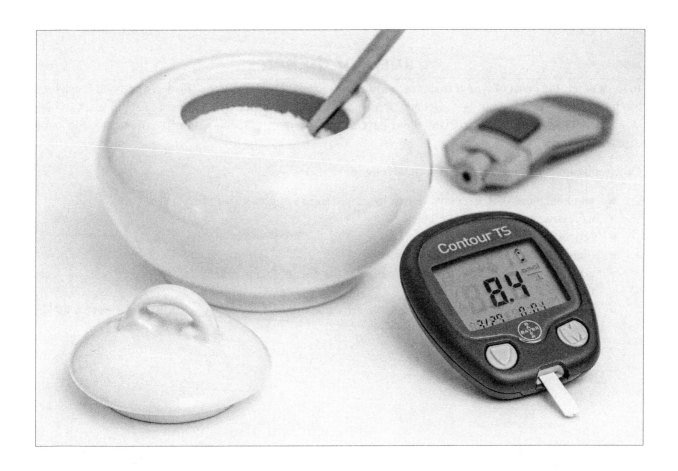

What is Diabetes?

Type II diabetes mellitus (T2DM) is a chronic disease characterized by high levels of glucose (sugar) in the blood (hyperglycemia). The pathology is due to an alteration in the quantity or functioning of insulin, a hormone produced by the cells of the pancreas. Insulin has the task of allowing circulating glucose to enter the body's cells, where it is then used as an energy source: if the pancreas does not produce a sufficient quantity of insulin (partial insulin deficiency) or if the organs target (muscle, liver, adipose tissue) do not respond adequately to the hormone, the body cannot use the circulating glucose as energy and therefore remains in the blood. As a result, glucose levels become increasingly high and cause damage to various organs, for example in the eyes (diabetic retinopathy), kidneys (diabetic nephropathy) and heart (coronary artery disease). Other complications given by the disease are numbness and tingling in the limbs (diabetic neuropathy), diabetic foot (foot ulcers) and complications of the neurovegetative system (erectile dysfunction). Furthermore, diabetes is often associated with other metabolic diseases such as arterial hypertension and dyslipidemia: in these cases we speak of metabolic syndrome. T2DM represents about 90% of all cases of diabetes, generally manifests itself in adulthood (about 2/3 of cases of diabetes affect people over 65), although in recent years an increasing number of cases are diagnosed in adolescence, a factor correlated to the increase in the incidence of childhood obesity. People with type II diabetes mellitus represent about 5% of the population, i.e. over 3 million people. However, it is estimated that about 1 million people with diabetes who do not yet know they have it may add to this number.

Causes of diabetes

In most cases, the onset of type II diabetes mellitus is associated with incorrect lifestyles and obesity, which often precedes it and is its trigger. Genetic predisposition can favor the development of the disease, which is why people suffering from T2DM often have close relatives (parents, siblings) affected by the same disease.

Other conditions that increase the risk of developing diabetes are:

- an unbalanced diet, excessively rich in simple sugars and fats;
- excessive consumption of alcohol;
- sedentary lifestyle;
- diabetes gestational;
- advanced age, T2DM generally occurs after the age of 40 and mainly affects people over 64 years of age;
- ethnicity, as populations in sub-Saharan Africa and the Middle East – North Africa have a higher risk of developing the disease.

Signs and symptoms of diabetes

Typically, type II diabetes mellitus remains silent (asymptomatic) for many years because hyperglycemia develops gradually and, at least initially, the signs and symptoms of the disease are more difficult to identify. Then you can find:

- intense and persistent thirst
- frequent need for urinate;
- glycosuria, i.e. the loss of sugar in the urine;
- increase of hunger;
- blurry vision and sense of fatigue;
- increased infections of the genitals and urinary tract (e.g.cystitis);
- minor cuts or wounds that take longer to heal;
- erectile dysfunction and drynessvaginal.

Diabetes diagnosis

To diagnose type II diabetes mellitus, a blood test is required. The main diagnostic tests are:

- blood sugar in the morning after at least 8 hours of fasting (values equal to or greater than 126 mg/dl are considered indicative of diabetes);
- hemoglobin glycosylated (HbA1c), which provides an average assessment of blood sugar over the last 2-3 months and, if higher than 6.5%, may indicate the presence of diabetes;
- oral glucose load test (after assessing blood sugar, a drink containing 75 grams of glucose is made to drink and, 2 hours later, a blood sugar equal to or greater than 200 mg/dl indicates the presence of diabetes);
- glycemia values equal to or greater than 200 mg/dl found throughout the day should lead one to suspect the diagnosis of diabetes.

Treatment of diabetes

Diet is the basis of T2DM therapy, every diabetic must scrupulously follow the diet prescribed by their diabetes specialist. In fact, a healthy, varied and balanced diet plays a very important role in the treatment of diabetes and has the following main objectives:

- achieving and/or maintaining a weight desirable;
- prevention of hyper or hypoglycemia;
- the reduction of the risk of developing atherosclerosis and microvascular complications (retinopathy, renal failure).

In addition to diet therapy, type II diabetes mellitus can also include pharmacological treatments that the diabetologist must establish on the basis of the clinical situation and the different personal characteristics of each one. Type II diabetics on insulin therapy may require individualized diet therapies which are generally provided by the hospital Dietetics and Clinical Nutrition Services.

GENERAL DIETARY RECOMMENDATIONS

1. Reduce sugar consumption simple.
2. Limit your total fat intake to less than 30% of your calorie intake daily.
3. Limit your consumption of saturated fat to less than 10% of your calorie intake daily.
4. Hire more fiber, at least 15 g per 1000 kcal.
5. Choose foods with a low glycemic index.
6. Never skip breakfast.
7. Consume complete meals for lunch and dinner (carbohydrates + proteins + vegetables + fruit), avoiding periods of prolonged fasting.
8. Equally divide the total amount of complex carbohydrates (e.g. bread, pasta, rice, potatoes, etc.) into the three main meals.
9. Choose simple cooking methods, such as steaming, poached, baked, grilled, in a pressure cooker, stewed or boiling. Avoid breaded and fried foods, which require large quantities of oil to cook.

The three following chapters indicate the foods to avoid, to limit and those generally advisable in the presence of the disease, but not the frequency or quantity necessary for a balanced diet, which can and must only be prescribed by a specialist doctor.

FOOD NOT ALLOWED

- White sugar, brown sugar and fructose to sweeten drinks, sweet syrups such as maple or agave, possibly replacing them with sweeteners such as stevia.
- Honey and jam.
- Sweets and confectionery such as cakes, pastries, cookies, jellies, puddings, ice cream, popsicles, candies, etc.
- Fruit in syrup, candied fruit and fruit mustard.
- Sugary drinks or soft drinks such as cola, orange soda, tonic water, iced teas but also fruit juices fruit, as they naturally contain sugar (fructose) even if they bear the wording "no added sugar" on the packaging.
- Sauces containing sugar such as ketchup, barbecue sauce, etc.
- Fatty condiments such as butter, margarine, lard, cream, etc.
- Sausages such as sausage, salami, frankfurters, zampone, cotechino, etc.
- Spirits.

FOODS ALLOWED IN MODERATION

- Fruit, as it naturally contains sugar (fructose), respecting the quantities indicated in the specific diet for each diabetic. Limit sugary fruits, such as grapes, bananas, figs, persimmons, tangerines, etc., and those with a higher glycemic index, such as melon and watermelon, to occasional consumption. Instead, give preference to cherries, apples, pears, apricots, peaches, strawberries, plums, oranges and grapefruit. Remember that the degree of ripeness of the fruit modifies its glycemic index: the riper and sugarier it is, the higher its glycemic index will be.
- Chestnuts, which are not a fruit, potatoes, which are not vegetables, and corn. These foods are important sources of starch, so they replace bread, pasta, rice and other sources of complex

13

carbohydrates. They can be eaten occasionally as a first course. In particular, potatoes have a fairly high glycemic index and therefore their derivatives (mashed potatoes, gnocchi, etc.) should also be limited.

- Polished rice, foods made with rice flour and refined cereals in general (e.g. common white bread, breadsticks, crackers, rusks, etc.) have a high glycemic index, therefore they should be eaten in small quantities and not combined with the same meal.

- Salt, to reduce the amount added to dishes during and after cooking and limit the consumption of foods that naturally contain large quantities of it, such as canned foods or brine, stock cubes and meat extracts, soy-type sauces, etc. Instead of salt, to flavor the preparations, it is possible to use 3 teaspoons (15 g) of grated Grana Padano DOP every day, a cheese rich in calcium, good proteins with high biological value (including the 9 essential amino acids), vitamins of group B and antioxidants such as vitamin A , zinc and selenium .

- Oil Olive oil, to be added raw with a teaspoon and without exaggerating.

- Wine Red, about half a glass per meal due to the high caloric intake.

ALLOWED AND RECOMMENDED FOODS

- Vegetables, both raw and cooked (50/50 ratio), to be eaten in large portions especially for their important fiber content, but also for their vitamin, mineral and antioxidant content. Green leafy vegetables such as lettuce, spinach, cabbage, turnip tops, etc. are particularly recommended.
- Fish, fresh or frozen, to be eaten no less than two-three times a week.
- Pasta, barley, spelt, rice, couscous, barley bread, rye bread and other whole grain complex carbohydrates (e.g. whole grain pasta, whole grain bread, whole grain crackers, whole grain rusks, etc.) because they increase fiber intake and reduce glycemic peak. Cooking "al dente" reduces the glycemic index of pasta, as does consuming cold pasta.
- Legumes such as chickpeas, beans, lentils, peas, broad beans, etc., since they are an important source of vegetable protein (they are therefore to be eaten as a second course and not as a side dish). Although they contain a small percentage of carbohydrates, they have a low glycemic index and seem to reduce the peak glycemic. They can be eaten once or twice a week, even in combination with carbohydrates to form tasty unique dishes.
- Meat, both red and white, to be eaten no more than twice a week, coming from lean cuts and stripped of visible fat. Poultry should be eaten without the skin, because it is the part that contains the most fat.
- Lean cold cuts such as cooked or raw ham, bresaola, speck, roast turkey and chicken, without visible fat, to be eaten once or twice a week.
- Skimmed or semi-skimmed milk and yogurt, as they are foods with a low glycemic index.
- Cheeses, to be eaten two or three times a week as a second course and not as a "between meal". You can choose fresh (100 g) or seasoned (50 g)
- Spices and herbs aromatics, foods with a low glycemic index that help flavor preparations by reducing the consumption of salt.
- Water, preferably low in mineral content, at least 2 L per day.

Behavioral advice

- In the event of overweight or obesity, weight loss and abdominal circumference regularization are recommended (waist circumference values greater than 94 cm in men and 80 cm in women are associated with a "moderate" cardiovascular risk; values greater than 102 cm in men and 88 cm in women are instead associated with a "high" cardiovascular risk) and a reduction in fat mass. Remember that returning to a normal weight allows you to reduce not only blood sugar levels, but also other cardiovascular risk factors (arterial hypertension, hypercholesterolemia,hypertriglyceridemia).
- Make lifestyle more active (e.g. go to work on foot or by bicycle instead of by car, park far from your destination, avoid using the lift and taking the stairs, etc.).
- Practice physical activity at least three times a week (minimum 150 minutes weekly, optimal 300 minutes) both aerobic and muscle strengthening (anaerobic). Constant physical exercise gives beneficial effects to those suffering from diabetes, as well as being essential for eliminating excess fat and losing weight properly.
- Read product labels, especially to make sure of their sugar content. Beware of "sugar-free" products, as they are often high in fat and therefore high-calorie.
- Have regular blood tests and heart screenings (as directed by your doctor).

Practical advice

Those suffering from type 2 diabetes mellitus should include in their diet:

- a breakfast consisting of a cup of partially skimmed milk or a jar of low-fat yogurt + rusks or bread or cereals or dry biscuits + a medium-sized fruit (about 150 g), to be eaten preferably with the peel (if edible and well washed);
- lunch and dinner as complete meals, consisting of bread, pasta or rice (preferably cooked "al dente", using whole grains in about 50% of cases) + a second course (meat or fish or cheese or cold cuts or eggs or legumes) + vegetables + a fruit. Those who do not want to eat first and second courses can prepare single dishes based on carbohydrates and proteins such as pasta with tuna, rice or pasta with legumes, pasta with mozzarella and tomato, sandwich with roast beef, etc., always accompanied by vegetables and fruit;
- 2 snacks (one in the morning and one in the afternoon), or in the late evening if you are used to having dinner early (before 8.00 pm), based on fresh fruit, low-fat yogurt with a spoonful of sugar-free cereals or a glass of milk with a couple of rusks.

16

BREAKFAST RECIPE

1. Omelette with Spinach and Mushrooms

Preparation time: 10 minutes

Cook time: 10 minutes

Servings: 1

Ingredients:

- 2 eggs
- 1/4 cup sliced mushrooms
- 1/2 cup baby spinach
- 1 tbsp olive oil
- Salt and pepper to taste

Directions:

1. Whisk the eggs in a small bowl and season with salt and pepper.
2. Heat the olive oil in a small non-stick skillet over medium heat.
3. Add the sliced mushrooms and sauté for 2-3 minutes until they are tender.
4. Add the baby spinach to the skillet and cook for another 1-2 minutes until wilted.

5. Pour the beaten eggs into the skillet and cook for 2-3 minutes until the edges start to set.
6. Using a spatula, gently lift the edges of the omelette and let the uncooked eggs flow underneath.
7. Once the eggs are mostly set, fold the omelette in half and slide it onto a plate.
8. Serve hot.

Per serving: Calories: 252 | Fat: 21g | Carbohydrates: 3g | Protein: 14g | Fiber: 1g

2. Greek Yogurt with Mixed Berries and Nuts

Preparation time: 5 minutes

Servings: 1

Ingredients:

- 1/2 cup plain Greek yogurt
- 1/2 cup mixed berries (such as strawberries, blueberries, and raspberries)

- 1 tbsp chopped nuts (such as almonds, walnuts, or pecans)

Directions

1. Spoon the Greek yogurt into a bowl.
2. Top with mixed berries and chopped nuts.
3. Serve chilled.

Per serving: Calories: 204 | Fat: 8g | Carbohydrates: 17g | Protein: 18g | Fiber: 4g

3. Cinnamon Apple Oatmeal

Preparation time: 5 minutes

Cook time: 5 minutes

Servings: 1

Ingredients:

- 1/2 cup old-fashioned rolled oats
- 1/2 cup unsweetened almond milk
- 1/2 cup water
- 1 small apple, peeled and chopped
- 1/2 tsp ground cinnamon
- 1 tbsp chopped nuts (such as almonds, walnuts, or pecans)

Directions

1. In a small saucepan, bring the almond milk and water to a boil.
2. Add the rolled oats and reduce the heat to medium.
3. Add the chopped apple and ground cinnamon to the saucepan and stir to combine.
4. Cook for 3-5 minutes, stirring occasionally, until the oatmeal is thick and creamy.
5. Spoon the oatmeal into a bowl and top with chopped nuts.

6. Serve hot.

Nutritional Facts (per serving): Calories: 272 | Fat: 10g | Carbohydrates: 41g | Protein: 8g | Fiber: 8g.

4. Scrambled Eggs with Diced Tomatoes and Green Onions

Preparation time: 5 minutes

Cook time: 5 minutes

Servings: 1

Ingredients:

- 2 eggs
- 1/4 cup diced tomatoes
- 1 green onion, thinly sliced
- 1 tbsp olive oil
- Salt and pepper to taste

Directions

1. Crack the eggs into a small bowl and whisk them with a fork.
2. Heat the olive oil in a non-stick skillet over medium heat.
3. Add the diced tomatoes and green onions to the skillet and sauté for 1-2 minutes until they are slightly softened.
4. Pour the beaten eggs into the skillet and cook for 2-3 minutes, stirring occasionally, until the eggs are scrambled and cooked through.
5. Season with salt and pepper to taste.
6. Serve hot.

Per serving: Calories: 201 | Fat: 16g | | Carbohydrates: 3g | Protein: 12g | Fiber: 1g

5. Avocado Toast with Poached Egg

Preparation time: 10 minutes

Cook time: 5 minutes

Servings: 1

Ingredients:

- 1 slice of whole grain bread, toasted
- 1/2 ripe avocado, mashed
- 1 large egg
- 1 tsp white vinegar
- Salt and pepper to taste
- Optional toppings: sliced cherry tomatoes, chopped cilantro, hot sauce

Directions

1. Toast the slice of whole grain bread and spread the mashed avocado on top.
2. Fill a small saucepan with water and add the white vinegar. Bring to a simmer over medium heat.
3. Crack the egg into a small bowl.
4. Using a spoon, create a gentle whirlpool in the simmering water.
5. Pour the egg into the center of the whirlpool and cook for 3-4 minutes until the white is set and the yolk is still runny.
6. Use a slotted spoon to remove the poached egg from the water and place it on top of the avocado toast.
7. Season with salt and pepper to taste and add any optional toppings.
8. Serve hot.

Per serving: Calories: 268 | Fat: 19g | Carbohydrates: 16g | Protein: 10g | Fiber: 9g

6. High-fiber Cereal with Unsweetened Almond Milk and Sliced Banana

Preparation time: 5 minutes

Servings: 1

Ingredients:

- 1 cup high-fiber cereal
- 1 cup unsweetened almond milk
- 1 small banana, sliced

Directions

1. Pour the high-fiber cereal into a bowl.
2. Add the unsweetened almond milk and stir to combine.
3. Top with sliced banana.
4. Serve immediately.

Per serving: Calories: 225 | Fat: 6g | Carbohydrates: 44g | Protein: 7g | Fiber: 12g

7. Tofu and Vegetable Stir-Fry

Preparation time: 10 minutes

Cook time: 15 minutes

Servings: 4

Ingredients:

- 1 block of firm tofu, drained and cut into cubes
- 2 cups mixed vegetables (such as broccoli, bell peppers, snap peas, carrots)
- 2 cloves garlic, minced
- 1 tbsp sesame oil
- 2 tbsp low-sodium soy sauce
- 1 tbsp cornstarch

- 1/4 cup water
- Salt and pepper to taste

Directions:

1. Heat the sesame oil in a large skillet over medium-high heat.
2. Add the minced garlic and sauté for 1-2 minutes until fragrant.
3. Add the cubed tofu and mixed vegetables to the skillet and sauté for 5-7 minutes until the vegetables are tender and the tofu is slightly browned.
4. In a small bowl, whisk together the low-sodium soy sauce, cornstarch, and water.
5. Pour the soy sauce mixture into the skillet and stir to coat the tofu and vegetables.
6. Cook for an additional 1-2 minutes until the sauce has thickened.
7. Season with salt and pepper to taste.
8. Serve hot.

Per Serving: Calories: 160 | Fat: 8g | Carbohydrates: 11g | Protein: 13g | Fiber: 4g

8. Whole-Grain Pancakes with Sugar-Free Syrup

Preparation time: 10 minutes

Cook time: 10 minutes

Servings: 2-3

Ingredients:

- 1 cup whole-grain pancake mix
- 3/4 cup water
- 1/2 cup sugar-free syrup

Method of Preparation:

1. In a large bowl, whisk together the whole-grain pancake mix and water until smooth.
2. Heat a non-stick skillet over medium heat.
3. Pour 1/4 cup of the pancake batter into the skillet for each pancake.
4. Cook for 2-3 minutes on each side until golden brown.
5. Serve with sugar-free syrup.

Per Serving: Calories: 226 | Fat: 2g |Carbohydrates: 48g | Protein: 6g | Fiber: 6g

9. High-Fiber Cereal with Unsweetened Almond Milk and Sliced Banana:

Preparation time: 5 minutes

Cook time: 0 minutes

Servings: 1

Ingredients:

- 1 cup high-fiber cereal
- 1 cup unsweetened almond milk
- 1 medium banana, sliced

Directions

1. Pour the high-fiber cereal into a bowl.
2. Pour the unsweetened almond milk over the cereal.
3. Top with sliced banana.

Per Serving: Calories: 220 | Fat: 4g | Carbohydrates: 44g | Fiber: 10g | Sugar: 10g | Protein: 6g

10. Chia Seed Pudding with Almond Milk and Fresh Fruit

Preparation time: 10 minutes

Cook time: 0 minutes

Servings: 2

Ingredients:

- 1/4 cup chia seeds
- 1 cup unsweetened almond milk
- 1 teaspoon vanilla extract
- Fresh fruit, for topping

Directions

1. In a medium bowl, whisk together the chia seeds, almond milk, and vanilla extract.
2. Cover and refrigerate for at least 4 hours or overnight, until the pudding thickens.
3. To serve, divide the pudding between two bowls and top with fresh fruit.

Per Serving: Calories: 150 | Fat: 10g | Carbohydrates: 14g | Fiber: 9 | Sugar: 1g | Protein: 5g

11. Smoked Salmon and Cream Cheese on a Whole-Grain Bagel

Preparation time: 5 minutes

Cook time: 0 minutes

Servings: 1

Ingredients:

- 1 whole-grain bagel, sliced in half
- 2 tablespoons cream cheese
- 2 oz smoked salmon
- 1 tablespoon capers
- 2 slices red onion
- Fresh dill, for garnish

Method of Preparation:

1. Toast the bagel halves until lightly crispy.
2. Spread the cream cheese on both halves of the bagel.
3. Layer the smoked salmon on the bottom half of the bagel.
4. Sprinkle capers over the smoked salmon.
5. Add slices of red onion on top.
6. Garnish with fresh dill.
7. Close the sandwich with the top half of the bagel.
8. Serve and enjoy!

Per Serving: | Calories: 400 | Fat: 16g | Carbohydrates: 41g | Fiber: 6g | Sugar: 3g | Protein: 25g

12. Vegetable Frittata:

Preparation time: 15 minutes

Cook time: 20 minutes

Servings: 4

Ingredients:

6 large eggs

1/4 cup milk

Salt and pepper, to taste

1 tablespoon olive oil

1/2 onion, chopped

2 cloves garlic, minced

2 cups chopped vegetables (e.g. bell pepper, zucchini, mushrooms)

1/4 cup grated Parmesan cheese

Directions

1. Preheat the oven to 375°F (190°C).
2. In a large bowl, whisk together the eggs, milk, salt, and pepper until well combined.
3. Heat the olive oil in a large oven-safe skillet over medium heat.
4. Add the onion and garlic, and sauté for 2-3 minutes until softened.
5. Add the chopped vegetables and cook for another 5-7 minutes, or until tender.
6. Pour the egg mixture into the skillet, making sure the vegetables are evenly distributed.
7. Sprinkle the Parmesan cheese over the top.
8. Transfer the skillet to the oven and bake for 15-20 minutes, or until the frittata is set and golden brown.
9. Remove from the oven and let cool for a few minutes before slicing and serving.

Per Serving: Calories: 170 | Fat: 11g | Carbohydrates: 7g | Fiber: 2g | Sugar: 3g | Protein: 12g

13. Low-Carb Breakfast Burrito with Scrambled Eggs, Cheese, and Salsa Wrapped in a Whole-Grain Tortilla:

Preparation time: 10 minutes

Cook time: 10 minutes

Servings: 1

Ingredients:

2 large eggs

1 tablespoon butter

Salt and pepper, to taste

1/4 cup shredded cheese

2 tablespoons salsa

1 whole-grain tortilla

Directions

1. In a small bowl, whisk together the eggs, salt, and pepper until well combined.
2. Heat the butter in a non-stick skillet over medium heat.
3. Add the egg mixture to the skillet and cook, stirring occasionally, until scrambled and cooked through.
4. Remove from heat and sprinkle the shredded cheese over the top.
5. Spoon the salsa over the cheese.
6. Warm the tortilla in the microwave for 10-15 seconds.
7. Spoon the egg mixture onto the center of the tortilla.
8. Roll the tortilla up tightly, tucking in the sides as you go.
9. Serve and enjoy!

Per Serving: Calories: 380 | Fat: 25g | Carbohydrates: 18g | Fiber: 10g | Sugar: 3g | Protein: 22g

14. Quinoa Breakfast Bowl with Nuts and Seeds

Preparation time: 10 minutes

Cook time: 20 minutes

Servings: 2

Ingredients:

- 1/2 cup uncooked quinoa
- 1 cup water
- 1/4 cup chopped nuts (e.g. almonds, walnuts)
- 1/4 cup mixed seeds (e.g. pumpkin, sunflower)
- 1/2 teaspoon cinnamon
- 1/4 teaspoon salt
- 1 tablespoon honey
- 1/2 cup unsweetened almond milk

Directions

1. Rinse the quinoa in a fine-mesh strainer and transfer to a medium saucepan.
2. Add the water and bring to a boil.
3. Reduce the heat to low, cover, and simmer for 15-20 minutes, or until the water is absorbed and the quinoa is tender.
4. In a small skillet, toast the chopped nuts and mixed seeds over medium heat for 3-4 minutes, or until fragrant.
5. In a medium bowl, combine the cooked quinoa, toasted nuts and seeds, cinnamon, salt, honey, and almond milk.
6. Stir to combine.
7. Divide the mixture between two bowls.
8. Serve and enjoy!

Per Serving: Calories: 290 | Fat: 13g | Carbohydrates: 36g | Fiber: 5g | Sugar: 11g | Protein: 10g

15. Cottage Cheese with Sliced Peaches and Cinnamon

Preparation time: 5 minutes |

Cook time: 0 minutes |

Servings: 1

Ingredients:

- 1/2 cup low-fat cottage cheese
- 1/2 peach, sliced
- 1/4 teaspoon cinnamon

Directions

1. Spoon the cottage cheese into a bowl.
2. Top with the sliced peach.
3. Sprinkle the cinnamon over the top.
4. Serve and enjoy!

Per Serving: Calories: 100 Fat: 2g | Carbohydrates: 11g | Fiber: 1g | Sugar: 7g | Protein: 11g

16. Overnight Oats With Chia Seeds, Berries, And Almond Milk

This overnight oat recipe is a delicious and anti-inflammatory breakfast option, made with chia seeds, berries, and almond milk. Prep time: 5 minutes | Cook time: None (overnight soak) | Serving: 1 | Yield: 1 serving

Ingredients

- 1/2 cup rolled oats
- 1/4 cup chia seeds
- 1/2 cup mixed berries
- 1/2 cup unsweetened almond milk
- 1 tablespoon honey (optional)

Method of preparation

1. In a mason jar or airtight container, combine the rolled oats, chia seeds, mixed berries, and almond milk.

2. Stir to combine, then add the honey (if using) and stir again.

3. Cover and refrigerate overnight.

4. In the morning, give the oats a good stir, then enjoy!

Nutritional fact: Serving size : 1 | Calories: 348 |Fat: 15g | Saturated Fat: 1g | Cholesterol: 0mg | Sodium: 70mg | Carbohydrates: 44g | Fiber: 12g | Sugar: 12g | Protein: 12g

17. Green Smoothie With Spinach, Kale, Avocado, And Ginger

This green smoothie is packed with anti-inflammatory ingredients like spinach, kale, avocado, and ginger.

Prep time: 5 minutes | Cook time: None | Serving: 1 | Yield: 1 serving

Ingredients

- 1 cup baby spinach
- 1 cup kale
- 1/2 avocado
- 1/2 banana
- 1 inch piece of ginger
- 1 cup unsweetened almond milk

Method of preparation

1. In a blender, combine the spinach, kale, avocado, banana, ginger, and almond milk.

2. Blend until smooth and creamy.

3. Serve immediately and enjoy!

Nutritional fact: Serving size : 1 | Calories: 256 | Fat: 15g | Saturated Fat: 2g | Cholesterol: 0mg | Sodium: 111mg | Carbohydrates: 27g | Fiber: 9g | Sugar: 7g | Protein: 6g

18. Turmeric Latte With Almond Milk And Honey

This turmeric latte is a comforting and anti-inflammatory drink made with almond milk and honey.

Prep time: 5 minutes | Cook time: 5 minutes | Serving: 1 | Yield: 1 serving

Ingredients

- 1 cup unsweetened almond milk
- 1 teaspoon turmeric powder
- 1/4 teaspoon ground cinnamon
- 1/4 teaspoon ground ginger
- 1 tablespoon honey

Method of preparation

1. In a small saucepan, heat the almond milk over medium heat.

2. Add the turmeric, cinnamon, and ginger, and stir to combine.

3. Bring the mixture to a simmer, then remove from heat.

4. Stir in the honey, then pour into a mug and enjoy!

Nutritional fact: Serving size : 1 | Calories: 103 | Fat: 7g | Saturated Fat: 0g | Cholesterol: 0mg | Sodium: 132mg | Carbohydrates: 11g | Fiber: 1g | Sugar: 8g

19. Quinoa Bowl With Veggies, Avocado, And A Poached Egg

This quinoa bowl is a healthy and anti-inflammatory breakfast option, made with quinoa, veggies, avocado, and a poached egg.

Prep time: 10 minutes | Cook time: 15 minutes | Serving: 1 | Yield: 1 serving

Ingredients

- 1/2 cup quinoa, cooked

- 1/2 cup diced vegetables of your choice (such as bell peppers, mushrooms, and onions)
- 1/2 avocado, diced
- 1 egg
- Salt and pepper, to taste

Method of preparation

1. In a pan, sauté the vegetables with salt and pepper until cooked.
2. On a plate, add cooked quinoa and sautéed vegetables.
3. In a separate pan, poach the egg by cracking it into a simmering water, cook for 2-3 minutes.
4. Add diced avocado and poached egg on top of quinoa mixture.
5. Serve hot and enjoy!

Nutritional fact: Serving size : 1 | Calories: 449 | Fat: 24g | Saturated Fat: 3g | Cholesterol: 186mg | Sodium: 31mg | Carbohydrates: 44g | Fiber: 12g | Sugar: 2g | Protein: 15g

20. Sweet Potato Toast With Almond Butter, Banana, And Cinnamon

This sweet potato toast is a delicious and anti-inflammatory breakfast option, made with sweet potato, almond butter, banana, and cinnamon.

Prep time: 5 minutes | Cook time: 10 minutes | Serving: 1 | Yield: 1 serving

Ingredients

- 1 sweet potato, sliced into 1/4 inch slices
- 1 tablespoon almond butter
- 1/2 banana, sliced
- 1/4 teaspoon ground cinnamon

METHOD OF PREPARATION

1. Preheat oven to 375°F (190°C).
2. Place sweet potato slices on a baking sheet and bake for 10-12 minutes, or until tender.
3. Remove from oven and spread almond butter on top of each slice.
4. Add banana slices and sprinkle with cinnamon.
5. Serve and enjoy!

Nutritional fact: Serving size : 1 | Calories: 285 | Fat: 12g | Saturated Fat: 1g | Cholesterol: 0mg | Sodium: 42mg | Carbohydrates: 42g | Fiber: 5g| Sugar: 13g | Protein: 5g

GRAINS, BEANS, AND LEGUME

1. Lentil soup with carrots and celery

Preparation time: 10 minutes

Cook time: 45 minutes

Servings: 4

Ingredients:

- 1 tablespoon olive oil
- 1 onion, chopped
- 2 cloves garlic, minced
- 2 carrots, chopped
- 2 celery stalks, chopped
- 1 cup brown or green lentils, rinsed and drained
- 4 cups vegetable broth or water
- 1 bay leaf
- 1 teaspoon dried thyme
- Salt and pepper, to taste
- Fresh parsley or cilantro, chopped, for garnish

Directions

1. Heat the olive oil in a large pot over medium heat.
2. Add the onion and garlic and sauté for 2-3 minutes, until softened.
3. Add the carrots and celery and sauté for another 5 minutes, until slightly softened.
4. Add the lentils, broth or water, bay leaf, thyme, salt, and pepper and bring to a boil.
5. Reduce heat to low and simmer for 35-40 minutes, or until the lentils are tender.
6. Remove the bay leaf and serve hot, garnished with fresh parsley or cilantro.

Per Serving: Calories: 203 | Fat: 4g | Saturated Fat: 1g | Cholesterol: 0mg | Sodium: 799mg | Carbohydrates: 31g | Fiber: 15g | Sugar: 6g| Protein: 14g

2. Black bean and vegetable stir-fry with brown rice

Preparation time: 10 minutes

Cook time: 20 minutes

Servings: 4

Ingredients:

- 1 tablespoon olive oil
- 1 onion, chopped
- 2 cloves garlic, minced
- 1 red bell pepper, sliced
- 1 green bell pepper, sliced
- 1 zucchini, sliced
- 1 yellow squash, sliced
- 1 cup cooked black beans, drained and rinsed
- 1 tablespoon soy sauce
- 1 tablespoon rice vinegar
- 1 teaspoon honey or agave nectar
- Salt and pepper, to taste
- 2 cups cooked brown rice, for serving

Method of preparation:

1. Heat the olive oil in a large skillet or wok over medium-high heat.
2. Add the onion and garlic and sauté for 2-3 minutes, until softened.
3. Add the bell peppers, zucchini, and yellow squash and stir-fry for 5-7 minutes, until slightly softened.
4. Add the black beans, soy sauce, rice vinegar, honey or agave nectar, salt, and pepper and stir-fry for another 2-3 minutes, until heated through.
5. Serve hot over brown rice.

Per Serving: Calories: 355 | Fat: 6g | Saturated Fat: 1g | Cholesterol: 0mg | Sodium: 337mg | Carbohydrates: 65g | Fiber: 12g | Sugar: 7g | Protein: 14g

3. Chickpea and spinach curry with quinoa

Preparation time: 10 minutes

Cook time: 25 minutes

Servings: 4

Ingredients:

- 1 tablespoon olive oil
- 1 onion, chopped
- 2 cloves garlic, minced
- 1 tablespoon curry powder
- 1 teaspoon ground cumin
- 1/2 teaspoon ground ginger
- 1/4 teaspoon cayenne pepper (optional)
- 1 can (15 oz) chickpeas, drained and rinsed
- 1 can (14.5 oz) diced tomatoes, undrained
- 2 cups fresh spinach leaves
- Salt and pepper, to taste
- 2 cups cooked quinoa, for serving

Directions

1. Heat the olive oil in a large skillet or saucepan over medium heat.
2. Add the onion and garlic and sauté for 2-3 minutes, until softened.
3. Add the curry powder, cumin, ginger, and cayenne pepper (if using) and sauté for another minute, until fragrant.
4. Add the chickpeas and diced tomatoes and bring to a simmer.
5. Reduce heat to low and simmer for 10-15 minutes, until the sauce has thickened slightly.
6. Add the spinach leaves and stir until wilted.
7. Season with salt and pepper to taste.
8. Serve hot over quinoa.

Per Serving: Calories: 346 | Fat: 7g | Saturated Fat: 1g | Cholesterol: 0mg | Sodium: 514mg | Carbohydrates: 58g | Fiber: 13g | Sugar: 7g | Protein: 15g

4. Tuna and white bean salad with whole-grain crackers

Preparation time: 10 minutes

Servings: 2

Ingredients:

- 1 can (5 oz) tuna, drained
- 1 can (15 oz) white beans, drained and rinsed
- 1 celery stalk, chopped
- 1/4 red onion, chopped
- 2 tablespoons chopped fresh parsley
- 1 tablespoon lemon juice
- 1 tablespoon olive oil
- Salt and pepper, to taste
- Whole-grain crackers, for serving

Directions:

1. In a medium bowl, combine the tuna, white beans, celery, red onion, and parsley.
2. In a small bowl, whisk together the lemon juice, olive oil, salt, and pepper.
3. Pour the dressing over the tuna and bean mixture and toss to combine.
4. Serve chilled with whole-grain crackers.

Per Serving: Calories: 361 | Fat: 11g | Saturated Fat: 2g | Cholesterol: 28mg | Sodium: 520mg | Carbohydrates: 38g | Fiber: 12g | Sugar: 1g | Protein: 29g

5. Mushroom and lentil shepherd's pie with mashed sweet potato topping

Preparation time: 15 minutes

Cook time: 50 minutes

Servings: 6

Ingredients:

- 1 tablespoon olive oil
- 1 onion, chopped
- 2 cloves garlic, minced
- 2 cups sliced mushrooms
- 1 cup brown or green lentils, rinsed and drained
- 2 cups vegetable broth or water
- 2 tablespoons tomato paste
- 2 tablespoons Worcestershire sauce
- Salt and pepper, to taste
- 4 cups mashed sweet potatoes (about 4 medium sweet potatoes)

Direction

1. Preheat the oven to 375°F (190°C).
2. Heat the olive oil in a large skillet over medium heat.
3. Add the onion and garlic and sauté for 2-3 minutes, until softened.
4. Add the mushrooms and sauté for another 5-7 minutes, until slightly softened.
5. Add the lentils, broth or water, tomato paste, Worcestershire sauce, salt, and pepper and bring to a boil.
6. Reduce heat to low and simmer for 25-30 minutes, until the lentils are tender and the liquid has mostly been absorbed.
7. Transfer the lentil mixture to a 9x13 inch baking dish.

8. Spread the mashed sweet potatoes over the lentil mixture.
9. Bake for 20-25 minutes, until the sweet potatoes are lightly browned on top.
10. Let cool for a few minutes before serving.

Per Serving: Calories: 281 | Fat: 4g | Fat: 1g | Cholesterol: 0mg | Sodium: 425mg | Carbohydrates: 55g | Fiber: 14g | Sugar: 13g | Protein: 9g

6. Red lentil and vegetable stew with barley

Preparation time: 10 minutes

Cook time: 40 minutes

Servings: 6

Ingredients:

- 1 tablespoon olive oil
- 1 onion, chopped
- 2 cloves garlic, minced
- 2 carrots, chopped
- 2 celery stalks, chopped
- 1 red bell pepper, chopped
- 1 cup red lentils, rinsed and drained
- 1 can (14.5 oz) diced tomatoes, undrained
- 4 cups vegetable broth
- 1/2 cup pearl barley
- 1 teaspoon dried thyme
- Salt and pepper, to taste

Directions

1. Heat the olive oil in a large pot over medium heat.
2. Add the onion and garlic and sauté for 2-3 minutes, until softened.

3. Add the carrots, celery, and red bell pepper and sauté for another 5-7 minutes, until slightly softened.
4. Add the lentils, diced tomatoes, vegetable broth, barley, thyme, salt, and pepper and bring to a boil.
5. Reduce heat to low and simmer for 30-35 minutes, until the vegetables and barley are tender.
6. Serve hot.

Per Serving: Calories: 227 | Fat: 3g | Saturated Fat: 0g | Cholesterol: 0mg | Sodium: 703mg | Carbohydrates: 42g | Fiber: 12g | Sugar: 7g | Protein: 11g

7. Mexican quinoa bowl with black beans, avocado, and salsa

Preparation time: 15 minutes | Cook time: 25 minutes | Servings: 4

Ingredients:

- 1 cup quinoa, rinsed and drained
- 1 can (15 oz) black beans, drained and rinsed
- 1 avocado, diced
- 1/2 cup salsa
- 1/2 red onion, chopped
- 1/2 cup chopped fresh cilantro
- 1 teaspoon chili powder
- 1/2 teaspoon cumin
- Salt and pepper, to taste

Directions

1. Cook the quinoa according to package instructions.
2. In a large bowl, combine the cooked quinoa, black beans, avocado, salsa, red onion, cilantro, chili powder, cumin, salt, and pepper.

3. Toss to combine.
4. Serve hot.

Per Serving: Calories: 308 | Fat: 11g | Saturated Fat: 1g | Cholesterol: 0mg | Sodium: 438mg | Carbohydrates: 45g | Fiber: 14g | Sugar: 2g | Protein: 12g

8. Chickpea and vegetable tagine with couscous

Preparation time: 15 minutes | Cook time: 40 minutes | Servings: 6

Ingredients:

- 1 tablespoon olive oil
- 1 onion, chopped
- 2 cloves garlic, minced
- 2 carrots, chopped
- 2 zucchini, chopped
- 1 red bell pepper, chopped
- 1 can (14.5 oz) diced tomatoes, undrained
- 1 can (15 oz) chickpeas, drained and rinsed
- 1 teaspoon ground cumin
- 1 teaspoon ground coriander
- 1 teaspoon ground cinnamon
- 1/2 teaspoon ground ginger
- 1/4 teaspoon cayenne pepper
- Salt and pepper, to taste
- 1/4 cup raisins
- 2 cups vegetable broth
- 1 cup couscous
- Chopped fresh cilantro, for garnish

Directions

1. Heat the olive oil in a large pot over medium heat.
2. Add the onion and garlic and sauté for 2-3 minutes, until softened.
3. Add the carrots, zucchini, and red bell pepper and sauté for another 5-7 minutes, until slightly softened.
4. Add the diced tomatoes, chickpeas, cumin, coriander, cinnamon, ginger, cayenne pepper, salt, and pepper and stir to combine.
5. Add the raisins and vegetable broth and bring to a boil.
6. Reduce heat to low and simmer for 25-30 minutes, until the vegetables are tender and the sauce has thickened.
7. While the tagine is simmering, cook the couscous according to package instructions.
8. Serve the tagine over the couscous, garnished with chopped cilantro.

Per Serving: Calories: 318 | Fat: 4g | Saturated Fat: 0g | Cholesterol: 0mg | Sodium: 575mg | Carbohydrates: 63g | Fiber: 12g | Sugar: 14g | Protein: 11g

9. White bean and kale soup with whole-grain bread

Preparation time: 15 minutes

Cook time: 35 minutes

Servings: 6

Ingredients:

- 1 tablespoon olive oil
- 1 onion, chopped
- 2 cloves garlic, minced
- 2 carrots, chopped
- 2 celery stalks, chopped
- 1 can (14.5 oz) diced tomatoes, undrained
- 2 cans (15 oz each) white beans, drained and rinsed

- 4 cups vegetable broth
- 1 bunch kale, stemmed and chopped
- 1 teaspoon dried thyme
- Salt and pepper, to taste
- Whole-grain bread, for serving

Directions

1. Heat the olive oil in a large pot over medium heat.
2. Add the onion and garlic and sauté for 2-3 minutes, until softened.
3. Add the carrots, celery, and diced tomatoes and sauté for another 5-7 minutes, until slightly softened.
4. Add the white beans, vegetable broth, kale, thyme, salt, and pepper and bring to a boil.
5. Reduce heat to low and simmer for 25-30 minutes, until the vegetables are tender and the kale is wilted.
6. Serve hot with whole-grain bread.

Per Serving: Calories: 246 | Fat: 4g | Saturated Fat: 0g | Cholesterol: 0mg | Sodium: 711mg | Carbohydrates: 42g | Fiber: 12g | Sugar: 5g | Protein: 14g

10. Lentil and vegetable chili with quinoa

Preparation time: 15 minutes

Cook time: 40 minutes

Servings: 6

Ingredients:

- 1 tablespoon olive oil
- 1 onion, chopped
- 2 cloves garlic, minced
- 2 carrots, chopped
- 1 red bell pepper, chopped
- 1 can (14.5 oz) diced tomatoes, undrained
- 1 cup brown lentils, rinsed and drained
- 2 cups vegetable broth
- 1 tablespoon chili powder
- 1 teaspoon ground cumin
- 1/2 teaspoon smoked paprika
- Salt and pepper, to taste
- 1 cup quinoa, rinsed and drained
- Chopped fresh cilantro, for garnish

Direction

1. Heat the olive oil in a large pot over medium heat.
2. Add the onion and garlic and sauté for 2-3 minutes, until softened.
3. Add the carrots and red bell pepper and sauté for another 5-7 minutes, until slightly softened.
4. Add the diced tomatoes, lentils, vegetable broth, chili powder, cumin, smoked paprika, salt, and pepper and stir to combine.
5. Bring to a boil, then reduce heat to low and simmer for 25-30 minutes, until the lentils are tender and the sauce has thickened.
6. While the chili is simmering, cook the quinoa according to package instructions.
7. Serve the chili over the quinoa, garnished with chopped cilantro.

Per Serving: Calories: 314 | Fat: 5g | Saturated Fat: 0g | Cholesterol: 0mg | Sodium: 629mg

Carbohydrates: 53g | Fiber: 16g | Sugar: 7g | Protein: 16g

11. Black bean and sweet potato enchiladas with whole-grain tortillas:

Preparation time: 20 minutes

Cook time: 40 minutes

Servings: 4

Ingredients:

1 large sweet potato, peeled and diced

1 can black beans, drained and rinsed

1/2 cup salsa

1 teaspoon chili powder

1 teaspoon ground cumin

Salt and pepper, to taste

4 whole-grain tortillas

1/2 cup shredded cheddar cheese

Direction

1. Preheat the oven to 375°F (190°C).
2. In a large bowl, mix together the sweet potato, black beans, salsa, chili powder, cumin, salt, and pepper.
3. Spread the mixture evenly over each tortilla and roll tightly.
4. Place the rolled tortillas in a baking dish and sprinkle with shredded cheddar cheese.
5. Bake for 20-25 minutes, until the cheese is melted and the enchiladas are heated through.
6. Serve with additional salsa and/or guacamole, if desired.

Per Serving: Calories: 355 | Fat: 8g | Saturated Fat: 3g | Cholesterol: 13mg | Sodium: 576mg | Carbohydrates: 56g | Fiber: 15g | Sugar: 6g | Protein: 16g

12. Chickpea and vegetable biryani with brown rice

Preparation time: 20 minutes

Cook time: 45 minutes

Servings: 4

Ingredients:

2 cups brown rice, rinsed and drained

1 can chickpeas, drained and rinsed

2 cups mixed vegetables (such as carrots, peas, green beans, and bell pepper), chopped

1 onion, chopped

2 cloves garlic, minced

1 tablespoon grated ginger

1 tablespoon curry powder

1 teaspoon ground cumin

Salt and pepper, to taste

2 cups vegetable broth

Chopped fresh cilantro, for garnish

Directions

1. Heat a large pot over medium heat and add the onion, garlic, and ginger. Sauté for 2-3 minutes, until fragrant.
2. Add the mixed vegetables and sauté for another 5-7 minutes, until slightly softened.
3. Add the chickpeas, curry powder, cumin, salt, and pepper and stir to combine.

4. Add the rice and vegetable broth and bring to a boil.
5. Reduce heat to low, cover, and simmer for 30-40 minutes, until the rice is tender and the liquid is absorbed.
6. Fluff the rice with a fork and sprinkle with chopped cilantro before serving.

Per Serving: Calories: 376 | Fat: 3g | Saturated Fat: 0g | Cholesterol: 0mg | Sodium: 450mg | Carbohydrates: 76g | Fiber: 11g | Sugar: 6g | Protein: 13g

13. Three-bean salad with red onion and vinaigrette dressing

Preparation time: 15 minutes

Cook time: 0 minutes

Servings: 6

Ingredients:

1 can kidney beans, drained and rinsed

1 can chickpeas, drained and rinsed

1 can black beans, drained and rinsed

1 red onion, chopped

1/4 cup apple cider vinegar

1/4 cup olive oil

1 tablespoon honey

1 teaspoon Dijon mustard

Salt and pepper, to taste

Chopped fresh parsley, for garnish

Direction

1. In a large bowl, mix together the kidney beans, chickpeas, black beans, and red onion.
2. In a separate bowl, whisk together the apple cider vinegar, olive oil, honey, Dijon mustard, salt, and pepper to make the vinaigrette dressing.
3. Pour the dressing over the bean mixture and toss to combine.
4. Chill in the refrigerator for at least 30 minutes before serving.
5. Garnish with chopped fresh parsley before serving.

Per Serving: Calories: 276 | Fat: 10g | Saturated Fat: 1g | Cholesterol: 0mg | Sodium: 374mg | Carbohydrates: 35g | Fiber: 10g | Sugar: 7g | Protein: 12g

14. Mediterranean lentil salad with feta cheese and whole-grain pita bread

Preparation time: 15 minutes

Cook time: 30 minutes

Servings: 4

Ingredients:

- 1 cup brown or green lentils, rinsed and drained
- 1 red bell pepper, chopped
- 1/2 cup chopped red onion
- 1/2 cup crumbled feta cheese
- 1/4 cup chopped fresh parsley
- 2 tablespoons olive oil
- 2 tablespoons lemon juice
- 1 clove garlic, minced
- Salt and pepper, to taste

- 4 whole-grain pita breads, cut into wedges

Directions

1. In a large pot, bring 4 cups of water to a boil.
2. Add the lentils and reduce heat to low. Simmer for 25-30 minutes, until the lentils are tender.
3. Drain any excess liquid from the lentils and transfer them to a large bowl.
4. Add the red bell pepper, red onion, feta cheese, and parsley to the bowl and toss to combine.
5. In a separate bowl, whisk together the olive oil, lemon juice, garlic, salt, and pepper to make the dressing.
6. Pour the dressing over the salad and toss to combine.
7. Serve with whole-grain pita bread wedges on the side.

Per Serving: Calories: 365 | Fat: 13g | Saturated Fat: 4g | Cholesterol: 17mg | Sodium: 364mg | Carbohydrates: 45g | Fiber: 15g | Sugar: 3g | Protein: 20g.

15. Black bean and corn salad with lime dressing and whole-grain tortilla chips

Preparation time: 15 minutes

16. Roasted Brussels Sprouts With Balsamic Vinegar

This is a healthy and flavorful side dish that combines the nuttiness of roasted Brussels sprouts with the tangy flavor of balsamic vinegar.

Prep Time: 10 minutes

Cook time: 0 minutes

Servings: 4

Ingredients:

- 1 can black beans, drained and rinsed
- 1 cup frozen corn kernels, thawed
- 1 red bell pepper, chopped
- 1/2 cup chopped red onion
- 1/4 cup chopped fresh cilantro
- 2 tablespoons olive oil
- 2 tablespoons lime juice
- 1 teaspoon honey
- Salt and pepper, to taste
- Whole-grain tortilla chips, for serving

Direction

1. In a large bowl, mix together the black beans, corn kernels, red bell pepper, red onion, and cilantro.
2. In a separate bowl, whisk together the olive oil, lime juice, honey, salt, and pepper to make the dressing.
3. Pour the dressing over the salad and toss to combine.
4. Serve with whole-grain tortilla chips on the side.

Per Serving Calories: 223 | Fat: 7g | Saturated Fat: 1g | Cholesterol: 0mg | Sodium: 211mg | Carbohydrates: 33g | Fiber: 9g | Sugar: 5g | Protein: 9g.

Cook Time: 25-30 minutes
Serving: 4
Yield: 4 servings

Ingredients:

- 1 pound Brussels sprouts, trimmed and halved
- 2 tablespoons olive oil
- 1 tablespoon balsamic vinegar
- Salt and pepper, to taste

Method of Preparation:

1. Preheat oven to 400 degrees F.
2. In a large bowl, combine the Brussels sprouts, olive oil, balsamic vinegar, salt, and pepper. Toss to evenly coat.
3. Spread the Brussels sprouts out on a baking sheet in a single layer.
4. Roast for 25-30 minutes or until tender and browned.

Serve and enjoy!

Nutritional facts (per serving):

Calories: 100 | Fat: 7g | Sodium: 20mg | Carbohydrates: 8g | Fiber: 3g | Protein: 3g

17. Spicy Roasted Cauliflower

This is a healthy and flavorful side dish that combines the mild flavor of cauliflower with a spicy kick.

Prep Time: 10 minutes
Cook Time: 20-25 minutes
Serving: 4
Yield: 4 servings

Ingredients:

- 1 head of cauliflower, cut into florets
- 2 tablespoons olive oil
- 1 teaspoon chili powder
- 1 teaspoon cumin
- Salt and pepper, to taste

Method of Preparation:

1. Preheat oven to 400 degrees F.
2. In a large bowl, combine the cauliflower, olive oil, chili powder, cumin, salt, and pepper. Toss to evenly coat.
3. Spread the cauliflower out on a baking sheet in a single layer.
4. Roast for 20-25 minutes or until tender and browned.
5. Serve and enjoy!

Nutritional facts (per serving):

Calories: 80 | Fat: 7g | Sodium: 20mg | Carbohydrates: 5g | Fiber: 2g | Protein: 1g

18. Garlic And Herb Roasted Carrots

This is a healthy and flavorful side dish that combines the sweetness of carrots with the flavor of garlic and herbs.

Prep Time: 10 minutes
Cook Time: 25-30 minutes
Serving: 4
Yield: 4 servings

Ingredients:

- 1 pound carrots, peeled and sliced
- 2 tablespoons olive oil
- 2 cloves of garlic, minced
- 1 teaspoon dried thyme
- 1 teaspoon dried rosemary
- Salt and pepper, to taste

Method of Preparation:

Preheat oven to 400 degrees F.

In a large bowl, combine the carrots, olive oil, garlic, thyme, rosemary, salt, and pepper. Toss to evenly coat.

Spread the carrots out on a baking sheet in a single layer.

Roast for 25-30 minutes or until tender and browned.

Serve and enjoy!

Nutritional facts (per serving): Calories: 100 | Fat: 7g | Sodium: 20mg | Carbohydrates: 12g | Fiber: 3g | Protein: 1g

19. Sautéed Kale With Garlic

This is a healthy and delicious side dish that combines the nutrient-rich kale with the flavor of garlic.

Prep Time: 5 minutes
Cook Time: 10 minutes

Serving: 4
Yield: 4 servings

Ingredients

1 bunch of kale, washed and chopped
2 tablespoons olive oil
2 cloves of garlic, minced
Salt and pepper, to taste

Method of preparation:

Heat the olive oil in a large skillet over medium heat.
Add the garlic and sauté for 1 minute.
Add the kale and sauté for 5-7 minutes or until wilted.
Stir in salt and pepper to taste.
Serve and enjoy!

Nutritional facts (per serving): Calories: 80 | Fat: 7g | Sodium: 40mg | Carbohydrates: 5g | Fiber: 1g | Protein: 2g

20. Grilled Eggplant With Basil And Mozzarella

This is a flavorful and healthy side dish that combines the meatiness of eggplant with the freshness of basil and the creaminess of mozzarella.

Prep Time: 15 minutes
Cook Time: 10-15 minutes
Serving: 4
Yield: 4 servings

Ingredients:

1 large eggplant, sliced into rounds
2 tablespoons olive oil
Salt and pepper, to taste
1/4 cup chopped fresh basil
1/4 cup shredded mozzarella cheese

Method of preparation:

Preheat a grill to medium-high heat.
Brush the eggplant slices with olive oil and season with salt and pepper.
Grill the eggplant slices for 5-7 minutes per side or until tender and grill marks appear.
Remove from grill and top each slice with basil and mozzarella cheese.
Serve and enjoy!

Nutritional facts (per serving):
Calories: 80 | Fat: 7g | Sodium: 20mg | Carbohydrates: 5g | Fiber: 2g | Protein: 2g

1. Spinach and Strawberry Salad with Feta Cheese and Balsamic Vinaigrette

Preparation time: 15 minutes

Servings: 4

Ingredients:

- 6 cups baby spinach
- 2 cups sliced strawberries
- 1/2 cup crumbled feta cheese
- 1/4 cup sliced almonds
- 1/4 cup balsamic vinegar
- 1/4 cup olive oil
- 1 tablespoon honey
- Salt and pepper to taste

Method of preparation:

1. In a large bowl, combine the spinach, strawberries, feta cheese, and sliced almonds.

2. In a small bowl, whisk together the balsamic vinegar, olive oil, honey, salt, and pepper to make the dressing.
3. Drizzle the dressing over the salad and toss to coat evenly.
4. Serve immediately.

Per Serving: Calories: 220\ | Fat: 18g | Carbohydrates: 13g | Fiber: 3g | Protein: 5g

2. Roasted Vegetable Salad with Mixed Greens and Goat Cheese

Preparation time: 15 minutes

Cook time: 30 minutes

Servings: 4

Ingredients:

- 4 cups mixed greens

- 1 red bell pepper, sliced
- 1 yellow bell pepper, sliced
- 1 zucchini, sliced
- 1 yellow squash, sliced
- 1/2 red onion, sliced
- 1 tablespoon olive oil
- Salt and pepper to taste
- 1/4 cup crumbled goat cheese
- 1/4 cup balsamic vinegar
- 1/4 cup olive oil
- 1 teaspoon Dijon mustard

Directions

1. Preheat the oven to 400°F (200°C).
2. In a large bowl, toss the sliced bell peppers, zucchini, yellow squash, and red onion with 1 tablespoon of olive oil, salt, and pepper.
3. Spread the vegetables in a single layer on a baking sheet and roast for 25-30 minutes, or until they are tender and slightly caramelized.
4. In a small bowl, whisk together the balsamic vinegar, 1/4 cup of olive oil, Dijon mustard, salt, and pepper to make the dressing.
5. In a large bowl, toss the mixed greens with the roasted vegetables and the dressing.
6. Top the salad with crumbled goat cheese.
7. Serve immediately.

Per Serving: Calories: 220 | Fat: 20g | Carbohydrates: 10g | Fiber: 3g | Protein: 4g

3. Broccoli and Cauliflower Salad with Raisins and Sunflower Seeds

Preparation time: 15 minutes

Servings: 4

Ingredients:

- 2 cups broccoli florets
- 2 cups cauliflower florets
- 1/2 cup raisins
- 1/2 cup sunflower seeds
- 1/2 cup plain Greek yogurt
- 1/4 cup mayonnaise
- 1 tablespoon apple cider vinegar
- 1 tablespoon honey
- Salt and pepper to taste

Directions

1. In a large bowl, combine the broccoli florets, cauliflower florets, raisins, and sunflower seeds.
2. In a small bowl, whisk together the Greek yogurt, mayonnaise, apple cider vinegar, honey, salt, and pepper to make the dressing.
3. Broccoli and Cauliflower Salad with Raisins and Sunflower Seeds (continued)
4. Drizzle the dressing over the salad and toss to coat evenly.
5. Serve immediately.

Per Serving: Calories: 290 | Fat: 20g | Carbohydrates:20g| Fiber: 4g | Protein: 9g

4. Caprese Salad with Fresh Basil and Balsamic Glaze

Preparation time: 10 minutes

Servings: 4

Ingredients:

- 2 large tomatoes, sliced
- 8 oz. fresh mozzarella cheese, sliced

- 1/4 cup fresh basil leaves
- 2 tablespoons balsamic glaze
- Salt and pepper to taste

Method of preparation:

1. On a large platter or individual plates, arrange the tomato slices, mozzarella slices, and fresh basil leaves in alternating layers.
2. Drizzle the balsamic glaze over the top of the salad.
3. Season with salt and pepper to taste.
4. Serve immediately.

Per Serving: Calories: 160 | Fat: 10g | Carbohydrates: 7g | Fiber: 1g | Protein: 12g

5. Greek Salad with Cucumber, Tomato, and Feta Cheese

Preparation time: 10 minutes

Servings: 4

Ingredients:

- 4 cups mixed greens
- 1 large cucumber, diced
- 2 large tomatoes, diced
- 1/2 red onion, sliced
- 1/2 cup crumbled feta cheese
- 1/4 cup olive oil
- 2 tablespoons red wine vinegar
- 1 tablespoon lemon juice
- 1 teaspoon dried oregano
- Salt and pepper to taste

Method of preparation:

1. In a large bowl, combine the mixed greens, diced cucumber, diced tomatoes, sliced red onion, and crumbled feta cheese.

2. In a small bowl, whisk together the olive oil, red wine vinegar, lemon juice, dried oregano, salt, and pepper to make the dressing.
3. Drizzle the dressing over the salad and toss to coat evenly.
4. Serve immediately.

Per Serving: Calories: 200 | Fat: 17g | Carbohydrates: 9g | Fiber: 2g | Protein: 5g

6. Arugula and Pear Salad with Walnuts and Blue Cheese

Preparation time: 10 minutes

Cook time: N/A

Servings: 4

Ingredients:

- 6 cups arugula
- 2 pears, thinly sliced
- 1/2 cup chopped walnuts
- 1/2 cup crumbled blue cheese
- 1/4 cup olive oil
- 2 tablespoons white wine vinegar
- 1 teaspoon Dijon mustard
- Salt and pepper to taste

Directions

1. In a large bowl, combine the arugula, sliced pears, chopped walnuts, and crumbled blue cheese.
2. In a small bowl, whisk together the olive oil, white wine vinegar, Dijon mustard, salt, and pepper to make the dressing.
3. Drizzle the dressing over the salad and toss to coat evenly.
4. Serve immediately.

Per Serving: Calories: 320 | Fat: 27g | Carbohydrates: 15g | Fiber: 4g | Protein: 8g

7. Kale and Quinoa Salad with Roasted Sweet Potato and Chickpeas

Preparation time: 15 minutes

Cook time: 30 minutes

Servings: 4

Ingredients:

- 2 cups cooked quinoa
- 1 large sweet potato, peeled and diced
- 1 can chickpeas, drained and rinsed
- 1 bunch kale, stems removed and leaves chopped
- 1/4 cup olive oil
- 2 tablespoons balsamic vinegar
- 1 teaspoon honey
- Salt and pepper to taste

Directions

1. Preheat the oven to 400°F (200°C).
2. In a large bowl, toss the diced sweet potato with 2 tablespoons of olive oil and season with salt and pepper to taste.
3. Spread the sweet potato on a baking sheet and roast for 20-25 minutes or until tender and golden brown.
4. In a large bowl, combine the cooked quinoa, roasted sweet potato, chickpeas, and chopped kale.
5. In a small bowl, whisk together the remaining 2 tablespoons of olive oil, balsamic vinegar, honey, salt, and pepper to make the dressing.
6. Drizzle the dressing over the salad and toss to coat evenly.

7. Serve immediately.

Per Serving: Calories: 410 | Fat: 17g | Carbohydrates: 54g | Fiber: 12g | Protein: 1

8. Grilled Vegetable Salad with Feta Cheese and Lemon Vinaigrette

Preparation time: 15 minutes

Cook time: 10 minutes

Servings: 4

Ingredients:

- 2 bell peppers, seeded and quartered
- 2 zucchinis, sliced lengthwise
- 1 eggplant, sliced into rounds
- 1/2 red onion, sliced
- 6 cups mixed greens
- 1/2 cup crumbled feta cheese
- 1/4 cup olive oil
- 2 tablespoons lemon juice
- 1 teaspoon honey
- Salt and pepper to taste

Directions

1. Preheat a grill or grill pan over medium-high heat.
2. In a large bowl, toss the bell peppers, zucchinis, eggplant, and red onion with 2 tablespoons of olive oil and season with salt and pepper to taste.
3. Grill the vegetables for 3-4 minutes per side or until tender and charred.
4. In a small bowl, whisk together the remaining 2 tablespoons of olive oil,
5. lemon juice, honey, salt, and pepper to make the dressing.

6. In a large bowl, combine the mixed greens and grilled vegetables.
7. Drizzle the dressing over the salad and toss to coat evenly.
8. Sprinkle the crumbled feta cheese over the top of the salad.
9. Serve immediately.

Per Serving: Calories: 280 | Fat: 21g | Carbohydrates: 18g | Fiber: 6g | Protein: 7g

9. Beet and Goat Cheese Salad with Mixed Greens and Honey Mustard Dressing

Preparation time: 15 minutes

Cook time: 1 hour (for roasting the beets)

Servings: 4

Ingredients:

1. 4 medium beets, roasted and sliced
2. 6 cups mixed greens
3. 1/2 cup crumbled goat cheese
4. 1/4 cup olive oil
5. 2 tablespoons apple cider vinegar
6. 1 tablespoon honey
7. 1 teaspoon Dijon mustard
8. Salt and pepper to taste

Direction

1. Preheat the oven to 400°F (200°C).
2. Wrap the beets in foil and roast them in the oven for 45-60 minutes or until tender.
3. Once the beets are cool enough to handle, peel and slice them.
4. In a large bowl, combine the mixed greens and sliced beets.

5. In a small bowl, whisk together the olive oil, apple cider vinegar, honey, Dijon mustard, salt, and pepper to make the dressing.
6. Drizzle the dressing over the salad and toss to coat evenly.
7. Sprinkle the crumbled goat cheese over the top of the salad.
8. Serve immediately.

Per Serving: Calories: 250 | Fat: 18g | Carbohydrates: 18g | | Fiber: 4g | Protein: 6g

10. Edamame and Vegetable Salad with Sesame Ginger Dressing

Preparation time: 10 minutes

Cook time: 5 minutes

Servings: 4

Ingredients:

- 2 cups shelled edamame
- 1 red bell pepper, seeded and diced
- 1 cup shredded carrots
- 1 cup diced cucumber
- 6 cups mixed greens
- 1/4 cup chopped scallions
- 1/4 cup olive oil
- 2 tablespoons rice vinegar
- 1 tablespoon soy sauce
- 1 tablespoon honey
- 1 tablespoon sesame oil
- 1 tablespoon grated fresh ginger
- Salt and pepper to taste

Method of preparation:

1. In a large bowl, combine the edamame, diced red bell pepper, shredded carrots, diced cucumber, mixed greens, and chopped scallions.
2. In a small bowl, whisk together the olive oil, rice vinegar, soy sauce, honey, sesame oil, grated ginger, salt, and pepper to make the dressing.
3. Drizzle the dressing over the salad and toss to coat evenly.
4. Serve immediately.

Per Serving: Calories: 320 | Fat: 21g| Carbohydrates: 24g | Fiber: 9g | Protein: 14g

11. Carrot and Raisin Salad with Greek Yogurt and Honey Dressing

Preparation time: 15 minutes

Servings: 4

Ingredients:

- 4 cups shredded carrots
- 1/2 cup raisins
- 1/4 cup chopped walnuts
- 1/2 cup plain Greek yogurt
- 2 tablespoons honey
- 1 tablespoon lemon juice
- 1/4 teaspoon ground cinnamon
- Salt and pepper to taste

Method of preparation:

1. In a large bowl, combine the shredded carrots, raisins, and chopped walnuts.
2. In a small bowl, whisk together the Greek yogurt, honey, lemon juice, cinnamon, salt, and pepper to make the dressing.

3. Drizzle the dressing over the salad and toss to coat evenly.
4. Serve immediately.

Per Serving: Calories: 180 | Fat: 6g | Carbohydrates: 29g | Fiber: 5g | Protein: 7g

12. Tomato and Cucumber Salad with Avocado and Lime Dressing

Preparation time: 10 minutes

Servings: 4

Ingredients:

- 2 cups cherry tomatoes, halved
- 2 cups diced cucumber
- 1 avocado, diced
- 1/4 cup chopped fresh cilantro
- 2 tablespoons olive oil
- 2 tablespoons lime juice
- 1 garlic clove, minced
- Salt and pepper to taste

Directions

1. In a large bowl, combine the cherry tomatoes, diced cucumber, diced avocado, and chopped cilantro.
2. In a small bowl, whisk together the olive oil, lime juice, minced garlic, salt, and pepper to make the dressing.
3. Drizzle the dressing over the salad and toss to coat evenly.
4. Serve immediately.

Per Serving: Calories: 140 | Fat: 11g | Carbohydrates: 10g | Fiber: 5g | Protein: 3g

13. Grilled Asparagus and Bell Pepper Salad with Balsamic Glaze

Preparation time: 10 minutes

Cook time: 10 minutes

Servings: 4

Ingredients:

- 1 pound asparagus, trimmed
- 1 red bell pepper, seeded and sliced
- 2 tablespoons olive oil
- Salt and pepper to taste
- 1/4 cup balsamic glaze

Directions

1. Preheat a grill or grill pan to medium-high heat.
2. In a large bowl, toss the trimmed asparagus and sliced red bell pepper with olive oil, salt, and pepper.
3. Grill the vegetables for 5-10 minutes or until tender and lightly charred.
4. In a large bowl, combine the grilled asparagus and bell pepper.
5. Drizzle the balsamic glaze over the vegetables and toss to coat evenly.
6. Serve immediately.

Per Serving: Calories: 90 | Fat: 7g | Carbohydrates: 7g | Fiber: 2g | Protein: 3g

14. Broccoli and Kale Slaw with Almonds and Cranberries

Preparation time: 15 minutes

Servings: 4

Ingredients:

- 4 cups thinly sliced broccoli florets
- 2 cups thinly sliced kale leaves
- 1/4 cup sliced almonds
- 1/4 cup dried cranberries
- 1/4 cup olive oil
- 2 tablespoons apple cider vinegar
- 2 tablespoons honey
- Salt and pepper to taste

Directions

1. In a large bowl, combine the thinly sliced broccoli florets and kale leaves.
2. Add the sliced almonds and dried cranberries to the bowl and toss to mix.
3. In a small bowl, whisk together the olive oil, apple cider vinegar, honey, salt, and pepper to make the dressing.
4. Drizzle the dressing over the salad and toss to coat evenly.
5. Serve immediately.

Per Serving: Calories: 250 | Fat: 19g | Carbohydrates: 19g | Fiber: 4g | Protein: 5g

15. Roasted Brussels Sprouts and Sweet Potato Salad with Maple Mustard Dressing

Preparation time: 15 minutes

Cook time: 25 minutes

Servings: 4

Ingredients:

- 1 pound Brussels sprouts, trimmed and halved
- 1 large sweet potato, peeled and diced
- 2 tablespoons olive oil
- Salt and pepper to taste
- 1/4 cup dried cranberries

- 1/4 cup chopped walnuts
- 2 tablespoons maple syrup
- 2 tablespoons Dijon mustard
- 2 tablespoons apple cider vinegar

Directions

1. Preheat the oven to 400°F.
2. In a large bowl, toss the halved Brussels sprouts and diced sweet potato with olive oil, salt, and pepper.
3. Spread the vegetables in a single layer on a baking sheet and roast for 25 minutes or until tender and lightly browned.
4. In a small bowl, whisk together the maple syrup, Dijon mustard, apple cider vinegar, salt, and pepper to make the dressing.
5. In a large bowl, combine the roasted Brussels sprouts and sweet potato with the dried cranberries and chopped walnuts.
6. Drizzle the dressing over the salad and toss to coat evenly.
7. Serve immediately.

Per Serving: | Calories: 250 | Fat: 13g | Carbohydrates: 33g | Fiber: 7g | Protein: 5g

16. Lentil And Butternut Squash Casserole

This lentil and butternut squash casserole is a healthy and anti-inflammatory option, made with lentils, butternut squash, and a blend of aromatic spices.
Prep time: 15 minutes |
Cook time: 45 minutes |
Serving: 4 |
Yield: 4 servings
Ingredients

- 1 cup green lentils, rinsed and drained
- 2 cups diced butternut squash
- 1 onion, diced
- 2 cloves of garlic, minced
- 1 teaspoon dried thyme
- 1/2 teaspoon ground black pepper
- 1/4 teaspoon red pepper flakes (optional)
- 1 cup vegetable broth
- Salt and pepper, to taste
- Toppings of your choice (such as shredded cheese, breadcrumbs, and chopped parsley)

Method of preparation

1. Pre heat the oven to 375°F (190°C).
2. In a large pot, sauté onion and garlic until softened.
3. Add the thyme, black pepper, and red pepper flakes (if using) and stir for a minute.
4. Add the lentils, vegetable broth, and butternut squash.
5. Bring to a boil, then reduce heat and let it simmer for 25 minutes or until lentils and butternut squash are cooked through.
6. Season with salt and pepper to taste.
7. Transfer the mixture to a baking dish and top with your choice of toppings.
8. Bake for 20 minutes or until toppings are golden brown.
9. Serve hot and enjoy!

Nutritional Fact: Serving size : 1 | Calories: 365 | Fat: 8g | Saturated Fat: 2g | Cholesterol: 0mg | Sodium: 516mg | Carbohydrates: 64g | Fiber: 14g | Sugar: 8g | Protein: 14g

17. Black Bean And Mushroom Enchiladas

These black bean and mushroom enchiladas are a healthy and anti-inflammatory option, made with black beans, mushrooms, and a homemade enchilada sauce.

Prep time: 15 minutes |
Cook time: 25 minutes |
Serving: 4 |
Yield: 4 servings

Ingredient

- 1 can black beans, rinsed and drained
- 2 cups diced mushrooms
- 1/2 cup diced red onion
- 1/4 cup chopped cilantro
- 8 corn tortillas
- 1/2 cup tomato sauce
- 1/4 cup chili powder
- 1 teaspoon ground cumin
- 1/4 teaspoon cayenne pepper
- Salt and pepper, to taste

Method of preparation

1. Preheat oven to 375°F (190°C).
2. In a large bowl, combine black beans, mushrooms, red onion, and cilantro.
3. In a separate bowl, mix together the tomato sauce, chili powder, cumin, cayenne pepper, and a pinch of salt and pepper.
4. Spread a spoonful of the enchilada sauce on each tortilla.
5. Add a spoonful of the black bean and mushroom mixture on top of the sauce.
6. Roll the tortillas and place them seam-side down in a baking dish.
7. Cover the enchiladas with the remaining enchilada sauce.
8. Bake for 25 minutes.
9. Serve hot and enjoy!

Nutritional Fact: Serving size : 2 enchiladas | Calories: 365 | Fat: 8g | Saturated Fat: 2g | Cholesterol: 0mg | Sodium: 516mg | Carbohydrates: 64g | Fiber: 14g | Sugar: 8g | Protein: 14g

18. Chickpea And Cauliflower Curry

This chickpea and cauliflower curry is a healthy and anti-inflammatory option, made with chickpeas, cauliflower, and a blend of aromatic spices.

Prep time: 10 minutes |
Cook time: 30 minutes |
Serving: 4 |
Yield: 4 servings

Ingredients

- 1 can chickpeas, rinsed and drained
- 2 cups diced cauliflower
- 1 onion, diced
- 2 cloves of garlic, minced
- 1 teaspoon ground cumin
- 1/2 teaspoon ground turmeric
- 1/4 teaspoon cayenne pepper
- 1/2 cup coconut milk
- Salt and pepper, to taste

Method of preparation

1. In a large pot, sauté onion and garlic until softened.
2. Add the cumin, turmeric, and cayenne pepper, and stir for a minute.
3. Add the cauliflower, chickpeas and coconut milk.
4. Bring to a boil then lower the heat and let it simmer for 20 minutes or until cauliflower is tender.
5. Season with salt and pepper to taste.
6. Serve hot over rice or with naan bread.

Nutritional Fact:
Serving size : 1 | Calories: 162 | Fat: 12g | Saturated Fat: 10g | Cholesterol: 0mg | Sodium: 516mg | Carbohydrates: 27g | Fiber: 8g | Sugar: 6g | Protein: 8g

19. Whole Grain And Bean Chili

This whole grain and bean chili is a healthy and anti-inflammatory option, made with whole grains, beans, and a blend of spices.

Prep time: 15 minutes |

Cook time: 1 hour |

Serving: 6 |

Yield: 6 servings

Ingredients

- 1 cup uncooked whole grains (such as quinoa, farro, or brown rice)
- 1 can black beans, rinsed and drained
- 1 can kidney beans, rinsed and drained
- 1 onion, diced
- 2 cloves of garlic, minced
- 1 can diced tomatoes
- 2 cups vegetable broth
- 1 tablespoon chili powder
- 1 teaspoon ground cumin
- 1/2 teaspoon smoked paprika
- Salt and pepper, to taste

Method of preparation

1. In a large pot, sauté onion and garlic until softened.
2. Add the chili powder, cumin, smoked paprika, and stir for a minute.
3. Add the diced tomatoes, vegetable broth, whole grains, black beans, and kidney beans.
4. Bring to a boil then lower the heat and let it simmer for 45 minutes or until the whole grains are cooked through.
5. Season with salt and pepper to taste.
6. Serve hot with your favorite toppings such as shredded cheese, sour cream, or avocado.

Nutritional Fact: Serving size : 1 | Calories: 365 | Fat: 8g | Saturated Fat: 2g Cholesterol: 0mg | Sodium: 516mg | Carbohydrates: 64g|| Fiber: 14g | Sugar: 8g | Protein: 14g

20. Red Lentil And Vegetable Soup

This red lentil and vegetable soup is a healthy and anti-inflammatory option, made with red lentils, mixed vegetables, and a blend of aromatic spices.

Prep time: 10 minutes |

Cook time: 30 minutes |

Serving: 4 | Yield: 4 servings

Ingredients

- 1 cup red lentils, rinsed and drained
- 2 cups mixed vegetables (such as carrots, celery, and onions)
- 1 onion, diced
- 2 cloves of garlic, minced
- 1 teaspoon dried thyme
- 1/2 teaspoon ground black pepper
- 1/4 teaspoon red pepper flakes (optional)
- 4 cups vegetable broth
- Salt and pepper, to taste

Method of preparation

1. In a large pot, sauté onion and garlic until softened.
2. Add the thyme, black pepper, and red pepper flakes (if using) and stir for a minute.
3. Add the vegetable broth, red lentils and mixed vegetables and bring to a boil.
4. Reduce heat and let it simmer for 25 minutes or until the lentils and vegetables are cooked through.
5. Season with salt and pepper to taste.
6. Serve hot with a piece of bread or crackers on the side.

Nutritional fact: Serving size : 1 | Calories: 162 | Fat: 12g | Saturated Fat: 10g | Cholesterol: 0mg | Sodium: 516mg | Carbohydrates: 27g | Fiber: 8g | Sugar: 6g | Protein: 8g

MEAT

1. Grilled Chicken with Roasted Vegetables

Preparation Time: 15 minutes

Cook Time: 25 minutes

Servings: 4

Ingredients:

- 4 chicken breasts
- 1 red bell pepper, sliced
- 1 yellow bell pepper, sliced
- 1 zucchini, sliced
- 1 red onion, sliced
- 2 tablespoons olive oil
- 1 tablespoon dried oregano
- Salt and pepper to taste

Directions

1. Preheat the grill to medium-high heat.
2. In a large bowl, combine sliced bell peppers, zucchini, and red onion with
3. olive oil, dried oregano, salt, and pepper. Toss to coat.
4. Grill chicken breasts for about 5-6 minutes per side or until the internal temperature reaches 165°F.
5. While the chicken is cooking, roast the vegetables in the oven at 400°F for about 20-25 minutes, until tender and slightly charred.
6. Serve the grilled chicken with the roasted vegetables on the side.

Per Serving: Calories: 320 | Fat: 12g | Protein: 42g | Carbohydrates: 12g | Fiber: 4g

2. Baked Salmon with Roasted Asparagus and Quinoa

Preparation Time: 10 minutes

Cook Time: 25 minutes

Servings: 4

Ingredients:

4 salmon fillets

1 pound asparagus, trimmed

1 cup quinoa

2 cups water

2 tablespoons olive oil

Salt and pepper to taste

Directions

1. Preheat the oven to 400°F.
2. Place salmon fillets on a baking sheet lined with parchment paper. Brush with olive oil and sprinkle with salt and pepper.
3. Roast the salmon in the oven for 15-20 minutes or until the internal temperature reaches 145°F.
4. Toss asparagus with olive oil, salt, and pepper, and place on a separate baking sheet. Roast in the oven for about 10-12 minutes or until tender and slightly charred.
5. Rinse quinoa in a fine mesh strainer and combine with water in a medium saucepan. Bring to a boil, then reduce heat to a simmer and cook for about 15-20 minutes or until the water is absorbed and the quinoa is tender.
6. Serve the baked salmon with roasted asparagus and quinoa on the side.

Per Serving: Calories: 395 | Fat: 16g | Protein: 33g | Carbohydrates: 29g | Fiber: 6g

3. Beef Stir-Fry with Vegetables and Soba Noodles

Preparation Time: 20 minutes

Cook Time: 15 minutes

Servings: 4

Ingredients:

- 1 pound flank steak, sliced thinly
- 1 red bell pepper, sliced
- 1 yellow bell pepper, sliced
- 1 onion, sliced
- 8 ounces soba noodles
- 3 tablespoons soy sauce
- 2 tablespoons hoisin sauce
- 1 tablespoon sesame oil
- 2 cloves garlic, minced
- Salt and pepper to taste

Directions

1. Cook soba noodles according to package instructions. Drain and set aside.
2. Heat sesame oil in a large wok or skillet over medium-high heat.
3. Add sliced flank steak to the skillet and cook for 2-3 minutes until browned. Remove from skillet and set aside.
4. Add sliced bell peppers and onion to the skillet and stir-fry for 3-4 minutes
5. Add minced garlic and stir-fry for an additional minute.
6. Add cooked soba noodles to the skillet with the vegetables and stir-fry for 1-2 minutes to combine.
7. In a small bowl, whisk together soy sauce and hoisin sauce. Pour over the stir-fry and add the cooked beef back to the skillet.
8. Stir-fry for an additional 1-2 minutes until heated through.
9. Serve hot.

Per Serving: Calories: 450 | Fat: 11g | Protein: 38g| Carbohydrates: 51g | Fiber: 4g

4. Turkey Chili with Kidney Beans and Quinoa

Preparation Time: 15 minutes

Cook Time: 40 minutes

Servings: 6

Ingredients:

- 1 pound ground turkey
- 1 onion, diced
- 1 red bell pepper, diced
- 3 cloves garlic, minced
- 1 can (14.5 ounces) diced tomatoes
- 1 can (15 ounces) kidney beans, drained and rinsed
- 1 cup quinoa
- 2 cups water or chicken broth
- 2 tablespoons chili powder
- 1 tablespoon cumin
- 1 teaspoon paprika
- Salt and pepper to taste

Directions

1. In a large pot, cook ground turkey over medium-high heat until browned, breaking it up into small pieces as it cooks.
2. Add diced onion, red bell pepper, and minced garlic to the pot and stir to combine.
3. Add diced tomatoes, kidney beans, quinoa, water or chicken broth, chili powder, cumin, paprika, salt, and pepper to the pot. Stir to combine.
4. Bring the chili to a boil, then reduce heat to low and simmer for 30-35 minutes, stirring occasionally, until the quinoa is cooked and the flavors have melded together.
5. Serve hot.

Per Serving: Calories: 320 | Fat: 9g | Protein: 24g | Carbohydrates: 37g | Fiber: 8g

5. Lemon Herb Roasted Chicken with Roasted Vegetables

Preparation Time: 15 minutes

Cook Time: 1 hour

Servings: 4

Ingredients:

- 1 whole chicken (3-4 pounds)
- 1 lemon, sliced
- 1 onion, sliced
- 3 cloves garlic, minced
- 1 pound baby potatoes, halved
- 1 pound carrots, peeled and sliced
- 2 tablespoons olive oil
- 1 tablespoon dried thyme
- 1 tablespoon dried rosemary
- Salt and pepper to taste

Directions

1. Preheat the oven to 375°F.
2. Place the chicken in a roasting pan. Stuff the cavity of the chicken with sliced lemon, onion, and minced garlic.
3. In a large bowl, toss baby potatoes and sliced carrots with olive oil, dried thyme, dried rosemary, salt, and pepper.
4. Arrange the vegetables around the chicken in the roasting pan.
5. Roast the chicken and vegetables in the oven for 50-60 minutes, or until the internal temperature of the chicken reaches 165°F and the vegetables are tender and slightly charred.

6. Let the chicken rest for 10 minutes before carving and serving.

Per Serving: Calories: 540 | Fat: 29g | Protein: 46g | Carbohydrates: 23g | Fiber: 5g

6. Grilled Shrimp Skewers with Mixed Greens and Quinoa

Preparation Time: 15 minutes

Cook Time: 10 minutes

Servings: 4

Ingredients:

- 1 pound large shrimp, peeled and deveined
- 1 tablespoon olive oil
- 1 tablespoon lemon juice
- 1 tablespoon honey
- 1 tablespoon Dijon mustard
- Salt and pepper to taste
- 4 cups mixed greens
- 1 cup cooked quinoa

Directions

1. Preheat grill to medium-high heat.
2. In a small bowl, whisk together olive oil, lemon juice, honey, Dijon mustard, salt, and pepper to make a marinade.
3. Thread shrimp onto skewers and brush with marinade.
4. Grill shrimp skewers for 3-4 minutes per side, or until shrimp are pink and slightly charred.
5. In a large bowl, toss mixed greens and cooked quinoa with remaining marinade.
6. Serve grilled shrimp skewers on top of mixed greens and quinoa salad.

Per Serving: Calories: 270 | Fat: 6g | Protein: 27g | Carbohydrates: 27g | Fiber: 3g

7. Baked Chicken Breast with Steamed Broccoli

Preparation Time: 10 minutes

Cook Time: 25 minutes

Servings: 4

Ingredients:

- 4 boneless, skinless chicken breasts
- 2 tablespoons olive oil
- 2 teaspoons garlic powder
- 2 teaspoons onion powder
- 2 teaspoons dried oregano
- Salt and pepper to taste
- 4 cups broccoli florets

Directions

1. Preheat the oven to 400°F.
2. Place chicken breasts in a baking dish and brush with olive oil.
3. Sprinkle garlic powder, onion powder, dried oregano, salt, and pepper over chicken breasts.
4. Bake chicken breasts in the oven for 20-25 minutes, or until the internal temperature reaches 165°F.
5. While chicken is baking, steam broccoli florets until tender.
6. Serve baked chicken breasts with steamed broccoli on the side.

Per Serving: Calories: 280 | Fat: 9g | Protein: 39g | Carbohydrates: 8g | Fiber: 3g

8. Pork Tenderloin with Roasted Sweet Potato and Green Beans

Preparation Time: 15 minutes

Cook Time: 30 minutes

Servings: 4

Ingredients:

- 1 pound pork tenderloin
- 2 tablespoons olive oil
- 2 teaspoons garlic powder
- 2 teaspoons dried thyme
- Salt and pepper to taste
- 2 large sweet potatoes, peeled and cubed
- 1 pound fresh green beans, trimmed

Directions

1. Preheat the oven to 400°F.
2. Place pork tenderloin in a baking dish and brush with olive oil.
3. Sprinkle garlic powder, dried thyme, salt, and pepper over pork tenderloin.
4. Add cubed sweet potatoes and trimmed green beans to the baking dish.
5. Drizzle vegetables with remaining olive oil and season with salt and pepper.
6. Roast pork tenderloin and vegetables in the oven for 25-30 minutes, or until pork is cooked through and vegetables are tender and slightly charred.
7. Let pork tenderloin rest for 5 minutes before slicing and serving with roasted sweet potato and green beans on the side.

Per Serving: Calories: 340 | Fat: 11g | Protein: 33g | Carbohydrates: 30g | Fiber: 8g

9. Beef and Vegetable Kebabs with Quinoa or Roasted Potatoes

Preparation Time: 20 minutes

Cook Time: 15 minutes

Servings: 4

Ingredients:

- 1 pound beef sirloin, cut into 1-inch cubes
- 2 tablespoons olive oil
- 2 tablespoons balsamic vinegar
- 2 teaspoons garlic powder
- 2 teaspoons dried oregano
- Salt and pepper to taste
- 1 red bell pepper, seeded and cut into 1-inch pieces
- 1 green bell pepper, seeded and cut into 1-inch pieces
- 1 red onion, cut into 1-inch pieces
- 4 cups cooked quinoa or roasted potatoes

Directions

1. Preheat grill to medium-high heat.
2. In a small bowl, whisk together olive oil, balsamic vinegar, garlic powder, dried oregano, salt, and pepper to make a marinade.
3. Thread beef cubes, bell peppers, and red onion onto skewers and brush with marinade.
4. Grill beef and vegetable kebabs for 10-15 minutes, turning occasionally, or until beef is cooked to desired doneness and vegetables are slightly charred.
5. Serve beef and vegetable kebabs on top of cooked quinoa or roasted potatoes.

Per Serving: Calories: 410 | Fat: 18g | Protein: 37g | Carbohydrates: 24g | Fiber: 4g

10. Turkey and Vegetable Stir-Fry with Soba Noodles

Preparation Time: 15 minutes

Cook Time: 15 minutes

Servings: 4

Ingredients:

- 1 pound ground turkey
- 2 tablespoons vegetable oil
- 1 tablespoon minced garlic
- 1 tablespoon minced ginger
- 2 cups mixed vegetables (such as broccoli, carrots, and snow peas)
- 1/4 cup soy sauce
- 1 tablespoon honey
- 1 tablespoon cornstarch
- 8 ounces soba noodles, cooked according to package instructions

Directions

1. In a large skillet or wok, heat vegetable oil over medium-high heat.
2. Add ground turkey and cook until browned and cooked through, breaking up any large chunks with a spatula.
3. Add minced garlic and minced ginger to the skillet and stir-fry for 1-2 minutes, until fragrant.
4. Add mixed vegetables to the skillet and stir-fry for 3-5 minutes, until tender.
5. In a small bowl, whisk together soy sauce, honey, and cornstarch to make a sauce.
6. Pour sauce over turkey and vegetables in the skillet and stir-fry for 2-3 minutes, until sauce has thickened and coated the turkey and vegetables.
7. Serve turkey and vegetable stir-fry over cooked soba noodles.

Per Serving: Calories: 480 | Fat: 14g | Protein: 34g | Carbohydrates: 58g | Fiber: 4g

11. Roasted Pork Loin with Brussels Sprouts and Sweet Potato

Preparation Time: 20 minutes

Cook Time: 1 hour

Servings: 6

Ingredients:

3-pound boneless pork loin

1 pound Brussels sprouts, trimmed and halved

2 large sweet potatoes, peeled and cubed

2 tablespoons olive oil

1 tablespoon dried thyme

1 tablespoon garlic powder

Salt and pepper to taste

Directions

1. Preheat oven to 375°F.
2. Place pork loin in a large roasting pan and season with salt, pepper, garlic powder, and dried thyme.
3. Toss Brussels sprouts and sweet potatoes with olive oil in a bowl and season with salt and pepper.

4. Arrange Brussels sprouts and sweet potatoes around the pork loin in the roasting pan.
5. Roast in the preheated oven for 1 hour, or until pork is cooked through and vegetables are tender.
6. Let pork rest for 10 minutes before slicing and serving with roasted Brussels sprouts and sweet potatoes.

Per Serving: Calories: 395 | Fat: 13g | Protein: 49g | Carbohydrates: 23g | Fiber: 6g

12. Baked Salmon with Roasted Brussels Sprouts

Preparation Time: 15 minutes

Cook Time: 25 minutes

Servings: 4

Ingredients:

- 4 salmon fillets
- 1 pound Brussels sprouts, trimmed and halved
- 2 tablespoons olive oil
- Salt and pepper to taste

Directions

1. Preheat oven to 400°F.
2. Place salmon fillets in a large baking dish and season with salt and pepper.
3. Toss Brussels sprouts with olive oil in a bowl and season with salt and pepper.
4. Arrange Brussels sprouts around the salmon fillets in the baking dish.
5. Bake in the preheated oven for 25 minutes, or until salmon is cooked through and Brussels sprouts are tender.

6. Serve salmon fillets with roasted Brussels sprouts.

Nutritional Facts (per serving):

Calories: 360

Fat: 22g

Protein: 34g

Carbohydrates: 10g

Fiber: 4g

13. Grilled Chicken and Vegetable Kabobs with Quinoa or Roasted Potatoes

Preparation Time: 20 minutes

Cook Time: 15 minutes

Servings: 4

Ingredients:

1 pound boneless, skinless chicken breast, cut into 1-inch cubes

2 tablespoons olive oil

2 tablespoons balsamic vinegar

2 teaspoons dried oregano

Salt and pepper to taste

1 red bell pepper, seeded and cut into 1-inch pieces

1 green bell pepper, seeded and cut into 1-inch pieces

1 red onion, cut into 1-inch pieces

4 cups cooked quinoa or roasted potatoes

Directions

1. Preheat grill to medium-high heat.
2. In a small bowl, whisk together olive oil, balsamic vinegar, dried oregano, salt, and pepper to make a marinade.
3. Thread chicken cubes, bell peppers, and red onion onto skewers and brush with marinade.
4. Grill chicken and vegetable kabobs for 10-15 minutes, turning occasionally, or until chicken is cooked through and vegetables are slightly charred.
5. Serve chicken and vegetable kabobs on top of cooked quinoa or roasted potatoes.

Per Serving: Calories: 395 | Fat: 13g | Protein: 34g | Carbohydrates: 36g | Fiber: 5g

1. In a large skillet, heat olive oil over medium-high heat.
2. Add ground turkey and cook until browned, breaking it up into small pieces with a spoon.
3. Add chopped bell pepper, onion, zucchini, and yellow squash to the skillet and cook until vegetables are tender.
4. Add minced garlic, chili powder, ground cumin, salt, and pepper to the skillet and cook for 1-2 minutes, stirring frequently.
5. Serve ground turkey and vegetable mixture on top of cooked quinoa or roasted potatoes.

Per Serving: Calories: 420 | Fat: 16g | Protein: 34g | Carbohydrates: 38g | Fiber: 7g

14. Ground Turkey and Vegetable Skillet with Quinoa or Roasted Potatoes

Preparation Time: 15 minutes

Cook Time: 20 minutes

Servings: 4

Ingredients:

- 1 pound ground turkey
- 1 tablespoon olive oil
- 1 red bell pepper, seeded and chopped
- 1 yellow onion, chopped
- 1 zucchini, chopped
- 1 yellow squash, chopped
- 2 cloves garlic, minced
- 1 tablespoon chili powder
- 1 teaspoon ground cumin
- Salt and pepper to taste
- 4 cups cooked quinoa or roasted potatoes

Directions

15. Herb Roasted Beef with Roasted Root Vegetables

Preparation Time: 15 minutes

Cook Time: 45 minutes

Servings: 6

Ingredients:

- 2-pound beef roast (sirloin, round, or chuck)
- 2 tablespoons olive oil
- 2 teaspoons dried thyme
- 2 teaspoons dried rosemary
- Salt and pepper to taste
- 2 large carrots, peeled and chopped
- 2 parsnips, peeled and chopped
- 2 sweet potatoes, peeled and cubed
- 1 red onion, chopped

Directions

1. Preheat oven to 375°F.

2. Place beef roast in a large roasting pan and season with olive oil, dried thyme, dried rosemary, salt, and pepper.
3. Toss chopped carrots, parsnips, sweet potatoes, and red onion with olive oil in a bowl and season with salt and pepper.
4. Arrange vegetables around the beef roast in the roasting pan.
5. Roast in the preheated oven for 45 minutes, or until beef is cooked to

desired doneness and vegetables are tender.
6. Let beef rest for 10 minutes before slicing and serving with roasted root vegetables.

Per Serving: Calories: 345 | Fat: 14g | Protein: 38g | Carbohydrates: 16g | Fiber: 4g

16. Grilled Lamb With Yogurt And Cucumber

A delicious and flavorful brunch dish made with lamb marinated in a mixture of yogurt, lemon juice, and spices, then grilled to perfection and served with a cool and refreshing cucumber yogurt sauce.
Prep time: 10 minutes
Cook time: 15 minutes
Serving: 4 people
Yield: 4 servings

Ingredients
- 8 lamb chops
- 1 cup of plain yogurt
- 1/4 cup of lemon juice
- 2 cloves of minced garlic
- 1 tsp of ground cumin
- 1 tsp of ground coriander
- Salt and pepper, to taste
- For the cucumber yogurt sauce:
- 1 cup of plain yogurt
- 1/2 cup of grated cucumber
- 1 clove of minced garlic
- 1 tbsp of chopped fresh mint
- Salt and pepper, to taste

Method of preparation:
1. In a small mixing bowl, combine the yogurt, lemon juice, garlic, cumin, coriander, salt, and pepper.

2. Place the lamb chops in a plastic bag or a shallow dish and pour the marinade over the lamb.
3. Marinate the lamb in the refrigerator for at least 30 minutes or up to 2 hours.
4. Preheat the grill to medium-high heat.
5. Grill the lamb chops for 2-3 minutes per side or until cooked through.
6. Remove the lamb from the grill and let it rest for 5 minutes before serving.
7. To make the cucumber yogurt sauce, mix all the ingredients together in a small mixing bowl.
8. Serve the lamb hot with the cucumber yogurt sauce on the side. Enjoy!
Nutritional facts (per serving):
Calories: 280 | Fat: 18g | Protein: 18g | Carbohydrates: 12g | Fiber: 2g | Sugar: 6g

17. Roasted Pork Loin With Apples And Onions

A delicious and tender brunch dish made with pork loin, roasted with apples and onions for added flavor.
Prep time: 10 minutes
Cook time: 45 minutes
Serving: 4 people
Yield: 4 servings
Ingredients:
1 lb pork loin
2 apples, cored and sliced

2 onions, sliced
2 cloves of minced garlic
2 tbsp of olive oil
Salt and pepper, to taste

Method of preparation

1. Preheat the oven to 425 degrees F (220 degrees C).
2. Season the pork loin with garlic, salt and pepper.
3. Place pork loin in a roasting pan and surround with apples and onions.
4. Drizzle olive oil over the pork and the apples and onions.
5. Roast the pork in the preheated oven for 25-30 minutes per pound or until the internal temperature reaches 145-160°F (63-71°C).
6. Remove the pork from the oven and let it rest for 5 minutes before slicing.
7. Serve the pork hot and enjoy!

Nutritional facts (per serving):
Calories: 260 | Fat: 18g | Protein: 18g | Carbohydrates: 12g | Fiber: 2g | Sugar: 6g

18. Baked Chicken Thighs With Lemon And Herb

A delicious and healthy brunch dish made with chicken thighs, baked with lemon and herbs for added flavor.
Prep time: 10 minutes
Cook time: 45 minutes
Serving: 4 people
Yield: 4 servings

Ingredients:

- 4 chicken thighs
- 2 tbsp of lemon juice
- 2 cloves of minced garlic
- 1 tbsp of chopped fresh herbs (such as parsley, thyme, and rosemary)
- 2 tbsp of olive oil

- Salt and pepper, to taste

Method of preparation:

1. Preheat the oven to 425 degrees F (220 degrees C).
2. Season the chicken thighs with garlic, lemon juice, herbs, salt and pepper.
3. Place chicken thighs in a baking dish.
4. Drizzle olive oil over the chicken.
5. Bake in the preheated oven for 25-30 minutes or until the chicken is cooked through.
6. Remove the chicken from the oven and let it rest for 5 minutes before serving.
7. Serve the chicken hot and enjoy!

Nutritional facts (per serving):
Calories: 260 | Fat: 18g | Protein: 18g | Carbohydrates: 8g | Fiber: 2g | Sugar: 3g

19. Grilled Beef With Garlic And Rosemary

A flavorful and healthy brunch dish made with beef sirloin, marinated in a mixture of garlic and rosemary, then grilled to perfection.
Prep time: 10 minutes
Cook time: 15 minutes
Serving: 4 people
Yield: 4 servings

Ingredients:

- 1 lb of beef sirloin
- 2 cloves of minced garlic
- 1 tbsp of chopped fresh rosemary
- 2 tbsp of olive oil
- Salt and pepper, to taste

Method of preparation:

1. In a small mixing bowl, combine the minced garlic, rosemary, olive oil, salt, and pepper.

2. Place the beef sirloin in a plastic bag or a shallow dish and pour the marinade over it.
3. Marinate the beef in the refrigerator for at least 30 minutes or up to 2 hours.
4. Preheat the grill to medium-high heat.
5. Grill the beef sirloin for 4-5 minutes per side or until cooked to your desired doneness.
6. Remove the beef from the grill and let it rest for 5 minutes before slicing.
7. Serve the beef hot and enjoy!

Nutritional facts (per serving): Calories: 280 | Fat: 18g | Protein: 28g | Carbohydrates: 2g | Fiber: 0g | Sugar: 1g

20. Pan-seared Pork With Lemon And Oregano

A flavorful and healthy brunch dish made with pork tenderloin, pan-seared with lemon and oregano for added flavor.
Prep time: 10 minutes
Cook time: 15 minutes
Serving: 4 people
Yield: 4 servings

Ingredients:

- 1 lb of pork tenderloin, sliced
- 2 tbsp of lemon juice
- 1 tbsp of dried oregano
- 2 cloves of minced garlic
- 1 tbsp of olive oil
- Salt and pepper, to taste

Method of preparation:
1. In a small mixing bowl, combine the lemon juice, oregano, garlic, salt and pepper.
2. Heat a skillet over medium-high heat and add olive oil.
3. Add the pork slices and cook for 2-3 minutes per side or until browned.
4. Remove the pork from skillet and set it aside.
5. Add the lemon juice mixture to the skillet and stir until well combined.
6. Return the pork slices to skillet and toss to coat with the sauce.
7. Cook for an additional 1-2 minutes or until the pork is cooked through.
8. Serve the pork hot and enjoy!

Nutritional facts (per serving): Calories: 260 Fat: 8g | Protein: 34g | Carbohydrates: 2g | Fiber: 0g | Sugar: 1g

FISH AND SEAFOOD

1. Grilled Salmon with Roasted Asparagus and Quinoa

Preparation time: 10 minutes

Cook time: 25 minutes

Servings: 4

Ingredients:

- 4 salmon fillets (4-6 oz each)
- 1 pound asparagus, trimmed
- 1 cup quinoa
- 2 cups vegetable broth
- 2 tablespoons olive oil
- Salt and pepper to taste
- Lemon wedges, for serving

Directions

1. Preheat grill to medium-high heat.
2. In a medium saucepan, combine quinoa and vegetable broth. Bring to a boil, then reduce heat and let simmer for 15-20 minutes, until fully cooked.
3. Toss asparagus with olive oil, salt, and pepper. Arrange in a single layer on a baking sheet.
4. Grill salmon for 3-4 minutes on each side, or until fully cooked.
5. While the salmon is grilling, roast the asparagus in the oven at 400°F for 10-12 minutes, until tender.
6. Serve the salmon with a side of quinoa and roasted asparagus. Squeeze a lemon wedge over the salmon before serving.

Per Serving: Calories: 473 | Protein: 41g | Fat: 22g | Carbohydrates: 28g | Fiber: 6g

2. Baked Tilapia with Roasted Brussels Sprouts

Preparation time: 10 minutes

Cook time: 25 minutes

Servings: 4

Ingredients:

- 4 tilapia fillets (4-6 oz each)
- 1 pound Brussels sprouts, trimmed and halved
- 2 tablespoons olive oil
- 1 teaspoon garlic powder
- Salt and pepper to taste
- Lemon wedges, for serving

Directions

1. Preheat oven to 400°F.
2. Toss Brussels sprouts with olive oil, garlic powder, salt, and pepper. Arrange in a single layer on a baking sheet.
3. Bake for 20-25 minutes, until tender and browned.
4. Season tilapia fillets with salt and pepper. Place on a baking sheet and bake for 10-12 minutes, until fully cooked.
5. Serve the tilapia with a side of roasted Brussels sprouts. Squeeze a lemon wedge over the fish before serving.

Per Serving: Calories: 261 | Protein: 34g | Fat: 11g | Carbohydrates: 10g | Fiber: 4g

3. Pan-Seared Tuna with Steamed Green Beans

Preparation time: 10 minutes

Cook time: 10 minutes

Servings: 4

Ingredients:

- 4 tuna steaks (4-6 oz each)

- 1 pound green beans, trimmed
- 2 tablespoons olive oil
- Salt and pepper to taste
- Lemon wedges, for serving

Directions

1. Heat a large skillet over medium-high heat.
2. Season tuna steaks with salt and pepper. Add to the skillet and sear for 2-3 minutes on each side, or until desired doneness is reached.
3. While the tuna is cooking, steam green beans for 5-7 minutes, until tender.
4. Serve the tuna with a side of steamed green beans. Squeeze a lemon wedge over the tuna before serving.

Per Serving: Calories: 282 | Protein: 36g | Fat: 12g | Carbohydrates: 8g | Fiber: 4g

4. Shrimp and Vegetable Stir-Fry with Soba Noodles

Preparation time: 15 minutes

Cook time: 15 minutes

Servings: 4

Ingredients:

- 8 oz soba noodles
- 1 pound shrimp, peeled and deveined
- 1 red bell pepper, sliced
- 1 yellow bell pepper, sliced
- zucchini, sliced
- 1 1 tablespoon olive oil
- 2 cloves garlic, minced
- 1 tablespoon grated ginger
- 2 tablespoons low-sodium soy sauce
- 1 tablespoon honey
- 1 tablespoon cornstarch

- 1/4 cup water
- Salt and pepper to taste

Directions

1. Cook soba noodles according to package instructions. Drain and set aside.
2. In a large skillet or wok, heat olive oil over high heat.
3. Add garlic and ginger to the skillet and stir-fry for 30 seconds.
4. Add shrimp, bell peppers, and zucchini to the skillet and stir-fry for 3-4 minutes, until shrimp is fully cooked and vegetables are tender-crisp.
5. In a small bowl, whisk together soy sauce, honey, cornstarch, water, salt, and pepper.
6. Pour the sauce over the shrimp and vegetables and stir-fry for an additional 1-2 minutes, until the sauce thickens.
7. Serve the stir-fry with a side of cooked soba noodles.

Per Serving: Calories: 377 | Protein: 32g | Fat: 5g | Carbohydrates: 52g | Fiber: 5g

5. Grilled Shrimp Skewers with Mixed Greens and Quinoa

Preparation time: 10 minutes

Cook time: 10 minutes

Servings: 4

Ingredients:

- 1 pound large shrimp, peeled and deveined
- 2 tablespoons olive oil
- 2 tablespoons chopped fresh parsley
- 1 tablespoon lemon juice
- Salt and pepper to taste

- 1 cup cooked quinoa
- 4 cups mixed greens
- 2 tablespoons balsamic vinaigrette

Directions

1. Preheat grill to medium-high heat.
2. In a large bowl, whisk together olive oil, parsley, lemon juice, salt, and pepper.
3. Add shrimp to the bowl and toss to coat.
4. Thread shrimp onto skewers.
5. Grill shrimp skewers for 2-3 minutes on each side, until fully cooked.
6. In a separate bowl, toss mixed greens with balsamic vinaigrette.
7. Serve the shrimp skewers with a side of cooked quinoa and mixed greens.

Per Serving: Calories: 269 Protein: 29g | Fat: 10g | Carbohydrates: 17g | Fiber: 3g

6. Lemon garlic chicken with roasted vegetables

Preparation time: 10 minutes

Cook time: 30 minutes

Servings: 4

Ingredients:

- 4 boneless, skinless chicken breasts
- 2 tablespoons olive oil
- 2 cloves garlic, minced
- 1 tablespoon grated lemon zest
- 1 tablespoon lemon juice
- 1 teaspoon dried thyme
- Salt and pepper to taste
- 2 cups chopped mixed vegetables (such as broccoli, bell peppers, and carrots)

Directions

1. Preheat oven to 400°F.

2. In a small bowl, whisk together olive oil, garlic, lemon zest, lemon juice, thyme, salt, and pepper.
3. Place chicken breasts in a baking dish and pour the lemon garlic mixture over the chicken, making sure to coat evenly.
4. Arrange the chopped vegetables around the chicken in the baking dish.
5. Bake in the preheated oven for 25-30 minutes, until chicken is fully cooked and vegetables are tender.
6. Serve the chicken and vegetables hot.

Per Serving: Calories: 250 | Protein: 27g | Fat: 10g | Carbohydrates: 12g | Fiber: 3g

7. Baked Cod with Roasted Root Vegetables

Preparation time: 15 minutes

Cook time: 35 minutes

Servings: 4

Ingredients:

- 4 cod fillets
- 1 lb root vegetables (carrots, parsnips, turnips), peeled and chopped
- 1 tbsp olive oil
- 1 tsp dried thyme
- Salt and pepper to taste

Directions

1. Preheat oven to 400°F.
2. Arrange chopped root vegetables on a baking sheet.
3. Drizzle with olive oil and sprinkle with thyme, salt, and pepper.
4. Toss the vegetables to coat evenly.
5. Bake in the preheated oven for 20-25 minutes, until tender.

6. Season the cod fillets with salt and pepper.
7. Place the cod fillets on top of the roasted vegetables.
8. Bake for an additional 10-12 minutes, until the cod is fully cooked.
9. Serve the baked cod with the roasted root vegetables.

Per Serving: Calories: 197 | Protein: 28g | Fat: 7g | Carbohydrates: 8g | Fiber: 2g

8. Grilled Salmon with Roasted Zucchini and Eggplant

Preparation time: 15 minutes

Cook time: 15 minutes

Servings: 4

Ingredients:

4 salmon fillets

2 zucchinis, sliced

1 eggplant, sliced

2 tbsp olive oil

2 cloves garlic, minced

Salt and pepper to taste

Directions

1. Preheat grill to medium-high heat.
2. In a large bowl, toss sliced zucchinis and eggplant with olive oil, garlic, salt, and pepper.
3. Grill the vegetables for 5-7 minutes on each side, until tender.
4. Season the salmon fillets with salt and pepper.

5. Grill the salmon fillets for 3-4 minutes on each side, until fully cooked.
6. Serve the grilled salmon with the roasted zucchini and eggplant.

Per Serving: Calories: 303 | Protein: 32g | Fat: 18g | Carbohydrates: 8g | Fiber: 3g

9. Seared Scallops with Roasted Cauliflower

Preparation time: 10 minutes

Cook time: 25 minutes

Servings: 4

Ingredients:

- 1 lb sea scallops
- 1 head cauliflower, chopped into florets
- 2 tbsp olive oil
- 1 tsp smoked paprika
- Salt and pepper to taste

Directions

1. Preheat oven to 400°F.
2. Arrange chopped cauliflower on a baking sheet.
3. Drizzle with olive oil and sprinkle with smoked paprika, salt, and pepper.
4. Toss the cauliflower to coat evenly.
5. Bake in the preheated oven for 20-25 minutes, until tender and lightly browned.
6. Heat a non-stick skillet over medium-high heat.
7. Season the scallops with salt and pepper.
8. Sear the scallops in the skillet for 2-3 minutes on each side, until golden brown and fully cooked.

9. Serve the seared scallops with the roasted cauliflower.

Per Serving: Calories: 179 | Protein: 23g | Fat: 8g | Carbohydrates: 8g | Fiber: 3g

10. Poached Salmon with Steamed Broccoli

Preparation time: 15 minutes

Cook time: 15 minutes

Servings: 4

Ingredients:

4 salmon fillets

1 lb broccoli florets

4 cups water

1 lemon, sliced

Salt and pepper to taste

Directions

1. In a large saucepan, bring the water to a simmer.
2. Add the lemon slices and season with salt and pepper.
3. Gently place the salmon fillets in the simmering water.
4. Cover the saucepan and let the salmon poach for 10-12 minutes, until fully cooked.
5. In the meantime, steam the broccoli florets in a steamer basket over boiling water for 5-7 minutes, until tender.
6. Serve the poached salmon with the steamed broccoli.

Per Serving: Calories: 225 | Protein: 29g | Fat: 10g | Carbohydrates: 7g | Fiber: 3g

11. Grilled Shrimp and Vegetable Kabobs with Quinoa or Roasted Potatoes

Preparation time: 15 minutes

Cook time: 15 minutes

Servings: 4

Ingredients:

- 1 lb large shrimp, peeled and deveined
- 1 red bell pepper, seeded and chopped
- 1 yellow bell pepper, seeded and chopped
- 1 zucchini, chopped
- 1 red onion, chopped
- 1 lemon, juiced
- 2 tbsp olive oil
- Salt and pepper to taste
- 1 cup cooked quinoa or roasted potatoes

Directions

1. Preheat the grill to medium-high heat.
2. Thread the shrimp and chopped vegetables onto skewers.
3. In a small bowl, whisk together the lemon juice, olive oil, salt, and pepper.
4. Brush the shrimp and vegetable kabobs with the lemon-oil mixture.
5. Grill the kabobs for 3-4 minutes per side, until the shrimp are fully cooked.
6. Serve the grilled shrimp and vegetable kabobs with quinoa or roasted potatoes.

Per Serving: Calories: 284 | Protein: 27g | Fat: 10g | Carbohydrates: 21g | Fiber: 4g

12. Pan-Seared Salmon with Roasted Carrots and Parsnips

Preparation time: 10 minutes

Cook time: 25 minutes

Servings: 4

Ingredients:

4 salmon fillets

4 carrots, peeled and chopped

4 parsnips, peeled and chopped

2 tbsp olive oil

1 tsp dried thyme

Salt and pepper to taste

Directions

1. Preheat oven to 400°F.
2. Arrange chopped carrots and parsnips on a baking sheet.
3. Drizzle with olive oil and sprinkle with dried thyme, salt, and pepper.
4. Toss the vegetables to coat evenly.
5. Bake in the preheated oven for 20-25 minutes, until tender and lightly browned.
6. Season the salmon fillets with salt and pepper.
7. Heat a large skillet over medium-high heat.
8. Add the salmon fillets to the skillet and sear for 3-4 minutes per side, until fully cooked.
9. Serve the pan-seared salmon with the roasted carrots and parsnips.

Per serving: | Calories: 355 | Protein: 31g | Fat: 22g | Carbohydrates: 12g | Fiber: 4g

13. Broiled Halibut with Roasted Brussels Sprouts and Sweet Potato

Preparation time: 10 minutes

Cook time: 25 minutes

Servings: 4

Ingredients:

- 4 halibut fillets
- 1 lb Brussels sprouts, trimmed and halved
- 2 sweet potatoes, peeled and chopped
- 2 tbsp olive oil
- 1 tsp garlic powder
- Salt and pepper to taste

Directions

1. Preheat oven to 400°F.
2. Arrange halved Brussels sprouts and chopped sweet potatoes on a baking sheet.
3. Drizzle with olive oil and sprinkle with garlic powder, salt, and pepper.
4. Toss the vegetables to coat evenly.
5. Bake in the preheated oven for 20-25 minutes, until tender and lightly browned.
6. Season the halibut fillets with salt and pepper.
7. Preheat the broiler.
8. Place the halibut fillets on a broiler pan and broil for 3-4 minutes per side, until fully cooked.
9. Serve the broiled halibut with the roasted Brussels sprouts and sweet potato.

Per Serving: | Calories: 316 | Protein: 34g | Fat: 10g | Carbohydrates: 24g | Fiber: 7g

14. Shrimp and Vegetable Stir-Fry with Soba Noodles

Preparation time: 15 minutes

Cook time: 15 minutes

Servings: 4

Ingredients:

- 1 lb large shrimp, peeled and deveined
- 2 bell peppers (1 red and 1 yellow), seeded and chopped
- 1 onion, chopped
- 2 garlic cloves, minced
- 2 cups broccoli florets
- 2 cups sliced mushrooms
- 2 tbsp olive oil
- 2 tbsp low-sodium soy sauce
- 1 tbsp honey
- 1 tsp grated ginger
- 8 oz soba noodles, cooked according to package instructions

Directions

1. In a small bowl, whisk together the soy sauce, honey, and grated ginger.
2. Heat the olive oil in a large skillet over medium-high heat.
3. Add the chopped onion and minced garlic to the skillet and sauté for 1-2 minutes.
4. Add the chopped bell peppers, broccoli, and sliced mushrooms to the skillet and stir-fry for 5-6 minutes, until the vegetables are tender-crisp.
5. Add the shrimp to the skillet and stir-fry for 2-3 minutes, until fully cooked.
6. Pour the soy sauce mixture over the stir-fry and stir to coat evenly.
7. Serve the shrimp and vegetable stir-fry with cooked soba noodles.

Per Serving: Calories: 406 | Protein: 31g | Fat: 9g | Carbohydrates: 56g | Fiber: 6g

15. Grilled Swordfish with Roasted Root Vegetables

Preparation time: 15 minutes

Cook time: 25 minutes

Servings: 4

Ingredients:

- 4 swordfish steaks
- 4 carrots, peeled and chopped
- 4 parsnips, peeled and chopped
- 2 tbsp olive oil
- 1 tsp dried rosemary
- Salt and pepper to taste

Directions

1. Preheat oven to 400°F.
2. Arrange chopped carrots and parsnips on a baking sheet.
3. Drizzle with olive oil and sprinkle with dried rosemary, salt, and pepper.
4. Toss the vegetables to coat evenly.
5. Bake in the preheated oven for 20-25 minutes, until tender and lightly browned.
6. Season the swordfish steaks with salt and pepper.
7. Preheat the grill to medium-high heat.
8. Grill the swordfish steaks for 3-4 minutes per side, until fully cooked.
9. Serve the grilled swordfish with the roasted root vegetables.

Per Serving: Calories: 346 | Protein: 43g | Fat: 13g | Carbohydrates: 15g | Fiber: 5g

16. Grilled Salmon With Lemon And Herbs

Introduction: This grilled salmon dish is a healthy and anti-inflammatory option, made with fresh salmon, lemon, and a blend of herbs.

Prep time: 10 minutes |
Cook time: 10 minutes |
Serving: 4 | Yield: 4 servings

Ingredients

- 4 salmon fillets
- 2 tablespoons olive oil
- Juice of 1 lemon
- 2 cloves of garlic, minced
- 2 tablespoons chopped fresh herbs (such as parsley, thyme, or dill)
- Salt and pepper, to taste

Method of preparation

In a small bowl, mix together olive oil, lemon juice, garlic, herbs, salt and pepper.

1. Brush the mixture over the salmon fillets.
2. Preheat grill to medium-high heat. Grill the salmon for 6-8 minutes on each side, or until cooked through.
3. Serve hot, garnished with additional herbs and lemon wedges if desired.

Nutritional fact: Serving size : 1 | Calories: 365 | Fat: 8g | Saturated Fat: 2g | Cholesterol: 0mg | Sodium: 516mg | Carbohydrates: 64g | Fiber: 14g | Sugar: 8g | Protein: 14g

17. Baked Tilapia With Tomato And Olive Relish

This baked Tilapia dish is a healthy and anti-inflammatory option, made with fresh

Tilapia, Tomato, Olive relish and a blend of herbs.
Prep time: 10 minutes |
Cook time: 20 minutes |
Serving: 4 | Yield: 4 servings

Ingredients

- 4 Tilapia fillets
- 2 cups diced tomatoes
- 1/2 cup chopped olives
- 2 cloves of garlic, minced
- 2 tablespoons olive oil
- 2 tablespoons chopped fresh herbs (such as parsley, thyme, or basil)
- Salt and pepper, to taste

Method of preparation

1. Preheat oven to 375°F (190°C).
2. In a small bowl, mix together tomatoes, olives, garlic, olive oil, herbs, salt, and pepper.
3. Place Tilapia fillets in a baking dish and spoon the tomato mixture over the top.
4. Bake for 20 minutes or until Tilapia is cooked through.
5. Serve hot with additional herbs and lemon wedges if desired.

Nutritional fact: Serving size : 1 | Calories: 365 | Fat: 8g | Saturated Fat: 2g | Cholesterol: 0mg | Sodium: 516mg | Carbohydrates: 64g | Fiber: 14g | Sugar: 8g | Protein: 14g

18. Pan-seared Tuna With Wasabi Aioli

This pan-seared tuna dish is a healthy and anti-inflammatory option, made with fresh tuna, wasabi aioli, and a blend of herbs.
Prep time: 10 minutes |
Cook time: 10 minutes |
Serving: 4 | Yield: 4 servings

Ingredients

- 4 tuna steaks
- 2 tablespoons olive oil
- 2 tablespoons wasabi aioli
- 2 cloves of garlic, minced
- 2 tablespoons chopped fresh herbs (such as parsley, thyme, or cilantro)
- Salt and pepper, to taste

Method of preparation

1. In a small bowl, mix together wasabi aioli, garlic, herbs, salt and pepper.
2. Brush the mixture over the tuna steaks.
3. Heat olive oil in a pan over medium-high heat. Add the tuna steaks and cook for 2-3 minutes on each side, or until cooked to your desired level of doneness.
4. Serve hot, garnished with additional herbs and lemon wedges if desired.

Nutritional fact: Serving size : 1 | Calories: 365 | Fat: 8g | Saturated Fat: 2g | Cholesterol: 0mg | Sodium: 516mg | Carbohydrates: 64g | Fiber: 14g | Sugar: 8g | Protein: 14g

19. Salmon And Asparagus In Parchment Paper

This salmon and asparagus dish is a healthy and anti-inflammatory option, made with fresh salmon, asparagus, and a blend of herbs, all wrapped in parchment paper for easy cooking and clean up.
Prep time: 10 minutes |
Cook time: 15 minutes |
Serving: 4 | Yield: 4 servings

Ingredients

- 4 salmon fillets
- 8 asparagus spears
- 2 cloves of garlic, minced
- 2 tablespoons olive oil
- 2 tablespoons chopped fresh herbs (such as parsley, thyme, or dill)

- Salt and pepper, to taste
- 4 sheets of parchment paper

Method of preparation

1. Preheat oven to 375°F (190°C).
2. Cut four pieces of parchment paper, each about 12 inches long.
3. On each piece of parchment paper, place a salmon fillet and 4 asparagus spears.
4. In a small bowl, mix together garlic, olive oil, herbs, salt and pepper.
5. Brush the mixture over the salmon and sparagus.
6. Fold the parchment paper over the salmon and asparagus, and seal the edges by folding and creasing.
7. Place the parchment packets on a baking sheet and bake for 15 minutes or until the almon is cooked through.
8. Serve hot, with additional herbs and lemon wedges if desired.

Nutritional fact: Serving size : 1 | Calories: 365 | Fat: 8g | Saturated Fat: 2g | Cholesterol: 0mg | Sodium: 516mg | Carbohydrates: 64g | Fiber: 14g | Sugar: 8g | Protein: 14g

20. Grilled Shrimp Skewers With Lemon And Garlic

These grilled shrimp skewers are a healthy and anti-inflammatory option, made with fresh shrimp, lemon, and garlic.

Prep time: 10 minutes |
Cook time: 10 minutes |
Serving: 4 | Yield: 4 servings

Ingredients

1 pound large shrimp, peeled and deveined
2 cloves of garlic, minced
2 tablespoons olive oil
Juice of 1 lemon
Salt and pepper, to taste
4 skewers (if using wooden skewers, soak them in water for 30 minutes before using)

Method of preparation

1. In a small bowl, mix together garlic, olive oil, lemon juice, salt and pepper.
2. Thread the shrimp onto skewers.
3. Brush the mixture over the shrimp skewers.
4. Preheat grill to medium-high heat. Grill the shrimp skewers for 2-3 minutes on each side, or until shrimp are cooked through and pink.
5. Serve hot, garnished with additional herbs and lemon wedges if desired.

Nutritional fact: Serving size: 1 Calories: 365 | Fat: 8g | Saturated Fat: 2g | Cholesterol: 0mg | Sodium: 516mg | Carbohydrates: 64g | Fiber: 14g | Sugar: 8g | Protein: 14g.

1. Chicken and vegetable soup with quinoa

Preparation time: 15 minutes

Cook time: 40 minutes

Servings: 4

Ingredients:

- 1 pound boneless, skinless chicken breasts, cut into small pieces
- 1 onion, diced
- 2 cloves garlic, minced
- 2 carrots, chopped
- 2 stalks celery, chopped
- 1 cup chopped kale
- 1 cup cooked quinoa
- 6 cups chicken broth
- 1 teaspoon dried thyme
- Salt and pepper to taste

Directions

1. In a large pot or Dutch oven, heat some olive oil over medium heat. Add the chicken and cook until browned.
2. Add the onion and garlic and cook until soft and fragrant, about 3 minutes.
3. Add the carrots and celery and cook for another 5 minutes.
4. Add the chicken broth, thyme, salt, and pepper, and bring to a boil.
5. Reduce the heat to low, cover the pot, and simmer for 20-25 minutes or until the vegetables are tender.
6. Add the chopped kale and cooked quinoa and cook for another 5-10 minutes or until the kale is wilted and the soup is heated through.
7. Taste and adjust seasoning as needed before serving.

Per Serving: Calories: 306 | Fat: 6g | Carbohydrates: 26g | Protein: 36g | Sodium: 1125mg

2. Lentil and vegetable soup

Preparation time: 15 minutes

Cook time: 45 minutes

Servings: 4

Ingredients:

- 1 cup dried lentils, rinsed and drained
- 1 onion, chopped
- 2 cloves garlic, minced
- 2 carrots, chopped
- 2 stalks celery, chopped
- 1 zucchini, chopped
- 4 cups vegetable broth
- 1 teaspoon dried thyme
- Salt and pepper to taste

Direction:

1. In a large pot or Dutch oven, heat some olive oil over medium heat. Add the onion and garlic and cook until soft and fragrant, about 3 minutes.
2. Add the carrots, celery, and zucchini and cook for another 5 minutes.
3. Add the lentils, vegetable broth, thyme, salt, and pepper, and bring to a boil.
4. Reduce the heat to low, cover the pot, and simmer for 30-40 minutes or until the lentils are tender.
5. Taste and adjust seasoning as needed before serving.

Per Serving: Calories: 238 | Fat: 1g | Carbohydrates: 44g | Protein: 15g | Sodium: 925mg

3. Tomato and vegetable soup with chickpeas

Preparation time: 10 minutes

Cook time: 30 minutes

Servings: 4

Ingredients:

- 1 onion, chopped
- 2 cloves garlic, minced
- 2 carrots, chopped
- 2 stalks celery, chopped
- 1 zucchini, chopped
- 1 can diced tomatoes
- 1 can chickpeas, rinsed and drained
- 4 cups vegetable broth
- 1 teaspoon dried oregano
- Salt and pepper to taste

Method of preparation:

1. In a large pot or Dutch oven, heat some olive oil over medium heat. Add the onion and garlic and cook until soft and fragrant, about 3 minutes.
2. Add the carrots, celery, and zucchini and cook for another 5 minutes.
3. Add the diced tomatoes, chickpeas, vegetable broth, oregano, salt, and pepper, and bring to a boil.
4. Reduce the heat to low, cover the pot, and simmer for 20-25 minutes or until the vegetables are tender.
5. Taste and adjust seasoning as needed before serving.

Per Serving: Calories: 210 | Fat: 3g | Carbohydrates: 38g | Protein: 10g | Sodium: 985mg

4. Creamy cauliflower soup

Preparation time: 10 minutes

Cook time: 30 minutes

Servings: 4

Ingredients:

1 head cauliflower, chopped

1 onion, chopped

2 cloves garlic, minced

4 cups vegetable broth

1 cup milk

1/4 cup heavy cream

Salt and pepper to taste

Directions

1. In a large pot or Dutch oven, heat some olive oil over medium heat. Add the onion and garlic and cook until soft and fragrant, about 3 minutes.
2. Add the cauliflower and vegetable broth and bring to a boil.
3. Reduce the heat to low, cover the pot, and simmer for 20-25 minutes or until the cauliflower is tender.
4. Use an immersion blender or transfer the soup to a blender and blend until smooth.
5. Return the soup to the pot and stir in the milk and heavy cream. Heat over low heat until heated through.
6. Taste and adjust seasoning as needed before serving.

Per Serving: Calories: 155 | Fat: 8g | Carbohydrates: 17g | Protein: 7g | Sodium: 845mg

5. Carrot and ginger soup

Preparation time: 10 minutes

Cook time: 30 minutes

Servings: 4

Ingredients:

- 2 tablespoons butter
- 1 onion, chopped
- 2 cloves garlic, minced
- 6-8 large carrots, peeled and chopped
- 4 cups vegetable broth
- 1 tablespoon grated fresh ginger
- Salt and pepper to taste

Directions

1. In a large pot or Dutch oven, heat the butter over medium heat. Add the onion and garlic and cook until soft and fragrant, about 3 minutes.
2. Add the carrots and vegetable broth and bring to a boil.
3. Reduce the heat to low, cover the pot, and simmer for 20-25 minutes or until the carrots are tender.
4. Use an immersion blender or transfer the soup to a blender and blend until smooth.
5. Return the soup to the pot, stir in the grated ginger, and heat over low heat until heated through.
6. Taste and adjust seasoning as needed before serving.

Per Serving: Calories: 115 | Fat: 5g | Carbohydrates: 17g | Protein: 2g | Sodium: 955mg

6. Split pea soup with ham

Preparation time: 10 minutes

Cook time: 1 hour 30 minutes

Servings: 6

Ingredients:

- 1 pound dried split peas
- 1 ham hock

- 1 onion, chopped
- 2 cloves garlic, minced
- 3 carrots, peeled and chopped
- 3 celery stalks, chopped
- 8 cups water or chicken broth
- Salt and pepper to taste

Directions

1. Rinse the split peas and remove any debris or discolored peas.
2. In a large pot or Dutch oven, add the split peas, ham hock, onion, garlic, carrots, celery, and water or chicken broth.
3. Bring to a boil, reduce the heat to low, cover the pot, and simmer for 1 hour 30 minutes or until the split peas are tender and the soup is thick.
4. Remove the ham hock from the soup, shred the meat, and return it to the pot.
5. Taste and adjust seasoning as needed before serving.

Per Serving: Calories: 395 | Fat: 10g | Carbohydrates: 48g | Protein: 30g | Sodium: 1150mg

7. Mushroom and barley soup

Preparation time: 10 minutes

Cook time: 45 minutes

Servings: 6

Ingredients:

- 1 cup pearl barley
- 2 tablespoons olive oil
- 1 onion, chopped
- 2 cloves garlic, minced
- 1 pound mushrooms, sliced
- 6 cups vegetable broth

- Salt and pepper to taste

Directions

1. Rinse the barley and drain.
2. In a large pot or Dutch oven, heat the olive oil over medium heat. Add the onion and garlic and cook until soft and fragrant, about 3 minutes.
3. Add the mushrooms and cook until they release their liquid and become tender, about 5-7 minutes.
4. Add the barley and vegetable broth and bring to a boil.
5. Reduce the heat to low, cover the pot, and simmer for 35-40 minutes or until the barley is tender.
6. Taste and adjust seasoning as needed before serving.

Per Serving: Calories: 210 | Fat: 6g | Carbohydrates: 36g | Protein: 7g | Sodium: 995mg

8. Minestrone soup with vegetables and beans

Preparation time: 10 minutes

Cook time: 30 minutes

Servings: 6

Ingredients:

- 2 tablespoons olive oil
- 1 onion, chopped
- 2 cloves garlic, minced
- 3 carrots, peeled and chopped
- 3 celery stalks, chopped
- 1 zucchini, chopped
- 1 can diced tomatoes (14.5 oz)
- 4 cups vegetable broth

- 1 can kidney beans, drained and rinsed (15 oz)
- 1 cup small pasta
- Salt and pepper to taste
- Fresh basil and Parmesan cheese for serving (optional)

Directions

1. In a large pot or Dutch oven, heat the olive oil over medium heat. Add the onion and garlic and cook until soft and fragrant, about 3 minutes.
2. Add the carrots, celery, and zucchini and cook for another 5 minutes.
3. Add the diced tomatoes, vegetable broth, kidney beans, and pasta, and bring to a boil.
4. Reduce the heat to low, cover the pot, and simmer for 15-20 minutes or until the vegetables and pasta are tender.
5. Taste and adjust seasoning as needed before serving. Serve with fresh basil and grated Parmesan cheese, if desired.

Per Serving: Calories: 250 | Fat: 5g | Carbohydrates: 43g | Protein: 10g | Sodium: 880mg

9. Roasted butternut squash soup

Preparation time: 15 minutes

Cook time: 1 hour 15 minutes

Servings: 6

Ingredients:

- 1 large butternut squash, peeled, seeded, and cut into 1-inch pieces
- 1 onion, chopped
- 2 cloves garlic, minced

- 2 tablespoons olive oil
- 4 cups vegetable broth
- 1 teaspoon ground cinnamon
- 1/2 teaspoon ground nutmeg
- Salt and pepper to taste
- Heavy cream or coconut milk for serving (optional)

Directions

1. Preheat the oven to 400°F (200°C).
2. In a large bowl, toss the butternut squash, onion, garlic, and olive oil until well coated.
3. Spread the vegetables in a single layer on a baking sheet and roast for 45-50 minutes or until tender and lightly browned.
4. Transfer the roasted vegetables to a large pot or Dutch oven. Add the vegetable broth, cinnamon, and nutmeg, and bring to a boil.
5. Reduce the heat to low, cover the pot, and simmer for 15-20 minutes.
6. Use an immersion blender or transfer the soup to a blender and puree until smooth.
7. Taste and adjust seasoning as needed. Serve with a drizzle of heavy cream or coconut milk, if desired.

Per Serving: Calories: 170 | Fat: 6g | Carbohydrates: 29g | Protein: 3g | Sodium: 650mg

10. Roasted Butternut Squash Soup

Preparation time: 10 minutes

Cook time: 50 minutes

Servings: 4

Ingredients:

- 1 medium butternut squash, peeled, seeded, and cut into chunks
- 1 large onion, chopped
- 2 cloves garlic, minced
- 2 tablespoons olive oil
- 4 cups chicken or vegetable broth
- Salt and pepper, to taste
- 1/2 teaspoon ground cinnamon
- 1/4 teaspoon ground nutmeg
- 1/2 cup heavy cream (optional)

Directions

1. Preheat the oven to 400°F (200°C).
2. In a large bowl, toss the butternut squash with the onion, garlic, and olive oil. Spread the mixture out on a baking sheet and roast for 30-35 minutes, or until the vegetables are tender and caramelized.
3. Transfer the roasted vegetables to a large pot and add the broth. Bring the mixture to a simmer and cook for 10-15 minutes, or until the vegetables are very tender.
4. Use an immersion blender or transfer the mixture to a blender and blend until smooth.
5. Add the cinnamon, nutmeg, salt, and pepper and cook for another 5 minutes. If desired, stir in the heavy cream.
6. Serve hot and enjoy!

Per Serving: Calories: 234 | Fat: 16g | Carbohydrates: 21g | Protein: 4g | Fiber: 4g | Sodium: 900mg

11. Turkey and Vegetable Soup with Quinoa

Preparation time: 10 minutes

Cook time: 30 minutes

Servings: 4

Ingredients:

- 1 tablespoon olive oil
- 1 onion, chopped
- 2 carrots, peeled and chopped
- 2 celery stalks, chopped
- 2 cloves garlic, minced
- 4 cups chicken or vegetable broth
- 1 cup cooked quinoa
- 2 cups cooked turkey, shredded
- Salt and pepper, to taste
- 2 tablespoons chopped fresh parsley

Method of preparation:

1. Heat the olive oil in a large pot over medium heat. Add the onion, carrots, and celery and sauté for 5-7 minutes, or until the vegetables are tender.
2. Add the garlic and cook for another 30 seconds.
3. Add the broth, quinoa, and turkey to the pot and bring the mixture to a simmer. Cook for 10-15 minutes, or until the soup is heated through and the flavors have melded.
4. Season the soup with salt and pepper to taste.
5. Garnish with chopped parsley before serving.

Per Serving: Calories: 300 | Fat: 7g | Carbohydrates: 28g | Protein: 30g | Fiber: 5g | Sodium: 900m

12. Creamy Tomato Soup with Lentils

Preparation time: 10 minutes

Cook time: 40 minutes

Servings: 4

Ingredients:

1 tablespoon olive oil

1 onion, chopped

2 cloves garlic, minced

1 can (28 oz) crushed tomatoes

4 cups vegetable broth

1 cup cooked lentils

1/2 cup heavy cream

Salt and pepper, to taste

Fresh basil leaves, chopped, for garnish

Directions

1. Heat the olive oil in a large pot over medium heat. Add the onion and garlic and sauté for 5-7 minutes, or until the onion is translucent.
2. Add the crushed tomatoes and vegetable broth to the pot and bring to a simmer. Cook for 15-20 minutes.
3. Add the cooked lentils and heavy cream and simmer for another 10 minutes.
4. Use an immersion blender or transfer the mixture to a blender and blend until smooth.
5. Season with salt and pepper to taste and garnish with chopped basil before serving.

Per Serving: Calories: 295 | Fat: 11g | Carbohydrates: 38g | Protein: 12g | Fiber: 14g | Sodium: 1050mg

13. Broccoli and Cheese Soup:

Preparation time: 10 minutes

Cook time: 30 minutes

Servings: 4

Ingredients:

- 2 tablespoons butter
- 1 onion, chopped
- 2 cloves garlic, minced
- 2 cups chopped broccoli florets
- 4 cups vegetable broth
- 1 cup milk
- 1 cup shredded cheddar cheese
- Salt and pepper, to taste

Directions

1. Melt the butter in a large pot over medium heat. Add the onion and garlic and sauté for 5-7 minutes, or until the onion is translucent.
2. Add the chopped broccoli and vegetable broth to the pot and bring to a simmer. Cook for 15-20 minutes, or until the broccoli is very tender.
3. Use an immersion blender or transfer the mixture to a blender and blend
4. until smooth.
5. Return the mixture to the pot and stir in the milk and shredded cheddar cheese.
6. Heat the soup until the cheese is melted and the soup is heated through.
7. Season with salt and pepper to taste before serving.

Per Serving: Calories: 320 | Fat: 21g | Carbohydrates: 16g

Protein: 16g

Fiber: 3g

Sodium: 1075mg

14. Creamy Vegetable Soup with White Beans

Preparation time: 10 minutes

Cook time: 30 minutes

Servings: 4

Ingredients:

- 1 tablespoon olive oil
- 1 onion, chopped
- 2 cloves garlic, minced
- 4 cups vegetable broth
- 2 cups chopped mixed vegetables (such as carrots, celery, and bell peppers)
- 1 can (15 oz) white beans, drained and rinsed
- 1/2 cup heavy cream
- Salt and pepper, to taste

Directions

1. Heat the olive oil in a large pot over medium heat. Add the onion and garlic and sauté for 5-7 minutes, or until the onion is translucent.
2. Add the vegetable broth and mixed vegetables to the pot and bring to a simmer. Cook for 15-20 minutes, or until the vegetables are very tender.
3. Use an immersion blender or transfer the mixture to a blender and blend until smooth.
4. Return the mixture to the pot and stir in the white beans and heavy cream.
5. Heat the soup until the beans are heated through and the soup is hot.
6. Season with salt and pepper to taste before serving.

Per Serving: Calories: 305 | Fat: 16g | Carbohydrates: 30g | Protein: 10g | Fiber: 9g | Sodium: 1115mg

15. Chicken and Vegetable Soup with Barley

Preparation time: 10 minutes

Cook time: 50 minutes

Servings: 6

Ingredients:

1 tablespoon olive oil

1 onion, chopped

2 cloves garlic, minced

4 cups chicken broth

2 cups chopped mixed vegetables (such as carrots, celery, and bell peppers)

1/2 cup pearl barley

2 cups cooked and shredded chicken breast

Salt and pepper, to taste

Directions

1. Heat the olive oil in a large pot over medium heat. Add the onion and garlic and sauté for 5-7 minutes, or until the onion is translucent.
2. Add the chicken broth and mixed vegetables to the pot and bring to a simmer. Cook for 15-20 minutes, or until the vegetables are very tender.
3. Stir in the barley and shredded chicken and simmer for another 20-30 minutes, or until the barley is cooked through.
4. Season with salt and pepper to taste before serving.

Per Serving: Calories: 240 | Fat: 5g | Carbohydrates: 26g | Protein: 23g | Fiber: 6g | Sodium: 715mg

16. Lentil And Vegetable Soup

A hearty and healthy soup made with lentils, vegetables, and spices, simmered to create a satisfying and nutritious meal.

Prep time: 15 minutes
Cook time: 45 minutes
Serving: 6 people
Yield: 6 servings

Ingredients:

- 1 cup of green lentils, rinsed
- 1 onion, diced
- 2 cloves of garlic, minced
- 2 cups of diced carrots
- 2 cups of diced celery
- 2 cups of diced potatoes
- 4 cups of vegetable broth
- 2 cups of water
- 1 tsp of cumin powder
- 1 tsp of dried thyme
- Salt and pepper, to taste

Method of preparation:

1. In a large pot, sauté the onion and garlic in a little bit of oil until softened.
2. Add the lentils, carrots, celery, potatoes, broth, water, cumin, thyme, salt and pepper.
3. Bring the soup to a boil, then reduce the heat and simmer for 30-40 minutes or until the lentils and vegetables are tender.
4. Serve the soup warm and enjoy!

Nutritional facts (per serving): Calories: 210 | Fat: 1g | Protein: 11g | Carbohydrates: 41g | Fiber: 13g | Sugar: 6g

17. Sweet Potato And Black Bean Stew

A hearty and healthy stew made with sweet potatoes, black beans, and spices, simmered to create a satisfying and nutritious meal.

Prep time: 15 minutes
Cook time: 45 minutes
Serving: 6 people
Yield: 6 servings

Ingredients:

- 2 medium sweet potatoes, peeled and diced
- 1 onion, diced
- 2 cloves of garlic, minced
- 2 cups of diced bell pepper
- 2 cups of diced zucchini
- 2 cans of black beans, drained and rinsed
- 4 cups of vegetable broth
- 2 cups of water
- 1 tsp of cumin powder
- 1 tsp of chili powder
- Salt and pepper, to taste

Method of preparation:

1. In a large pot, sauté the onion and garlic in a little bit of oil until softened.
2. Add the sweet potatoes, bell pepper, zucchini, black beans, broth, water, cumin, chili powder, salt and pepper.
3. Bring the stew to a boil, then reduce the heat and simmer for 30-40 minutes or until the vegetables are tender.
4. Serve the stew warm and enjoy!

Nutritional facts (per serving):
Calories: 260 | Fat: 2g | Protein: 11g | Carbohydrates: 52g | Fiber: 12g | Sugar: 8g

18. Split Pea And Ham Soup

A hearty and comforting soup made with split peas, ham, and vegetables, simmered to create a satisfying and nutritious meal.

Prep time: 15 minutes
Cook time: 1 hour
Serving: 6 people
Yield: 6 servings

Ingredients:

- 1 cup of split peas, rinsed
- 1 onion, diced
- 2 cloves of garlic, minced
- 2 cups of diced carrots
- 2 cups of diced celery
- 2 cups of diced potatoes
- 4 cups of chicken broth
- 2 cups of water
- 1 lb of diced ham
- 1 tsp of dried thyme
- Salt and pepper, to taste

Method of preparation:

1. In a large pot, sauté the onion and garlic in a little bit of oil until softened.
2. Add the split peas, carrots, celery, potatoes, broth, water, ham, thyme, salt and pepper.
3. Bring the soup to a boil, then reduce the heat and simmer for 45-60 minutes or until the split peas and vegetables are tender.
4. Serve the soup warm and enjoy!

Nutritional facts (per serving):
Calories: 350 | Fat: 10g | Protein: 25g | Carbohydrates: 40g | Fiber: 10g | Sugar: 8g

19. Chicken And Vegetable Soup

A comforting and healthy soup made with chicken, vegetables, and spices, simmered to create a satisfying and nutritious meal.
Prep time: 15 minutes
Cook time: 45 minutes
Serving: 6 people
Yield: 6 servings

Ingredients:
- 2 cups of diced cooked chicken
- 1 onion, diced
- 2 cloves of garlic, minced
- 2 cups of diced carrots
- 2 cups of diced celery

- 2 cups of diced potatoes
- 4 cups of chicken broth
- 2 cups of water
- 1 tsp of dried thyme
- Salt and pepper, to taste

Method of preparation:

1. In a large pot, sauté the onion and garlic in a little bit of oil until softened.
2. Add the chicken, carrots, celery, potatoes, broth, water, thyme, salt and pepper.
3. Bring the soup to a boil, then reduce the heat and simmer for 30-40 minutes or until the vegetables are tender.
4. Serve the soup warm and enjoy!

Nutritional facts (per serving):
Calories: 210 | Fat: 5g | Protein: 18g | Carbohydrates: 22g | Fiber: 3g | Sugar: 6g

20. Moroccan Chicken Stew

A flavorful and healthy stew made with chicken, vegetables, and spices, simmered to create a satisfying and nutritious meal.
Prep time: 15 minutes
Cook time: 45 minutes
Serving: 6 people
Yield: 6 servings

Ingredients:
- 2 cups of diced cooked chicken
- 1 onion, diced
- 2 cloves of garlic, minced
- 2 cups of diced bell pepper
- 2 cups of diced zucchini
- 1 can of diced tomatoes
- 2 cups of chicken broth
- 2 cups of water
- 1 tsp of cumin powder
- 1 tsp of cinnamon powder
- 1 tsp of paprika powder
- Salt and pepper, to taste

Method of preparation:

1. In a large pot, sauté the onion and garlic in a little bit of oil until softened.
2. Add the chicken, bell pepper, zucchini, tomatoes, broth, water, cumin, cinnamon, paprika, salt and pepper.
3. Bring the stew to a boil, then reduce the heat and simmer for 30-40 minutes or until the vegetables are tender.
4. Serve the stew warm and enjoy!

Nutritional facts (per serving):

Calories: 210 | Fat: 5g | Protein: 18g | Carbohydrates: 22g | Fiber: 3g | Sugar: 6g

DESSERT

1. Fresh berries with whipped cream or Greek yogurt

Preparation time: 5 minutes

Servings: 4

Ingredients:

- 2 cups fresh mixed berries (such as strawberries, blueberries, and raspberries)
- 1 cup heavy whipping cream or Greek yogurt
- 1 tablespoon granulated sugar (optional)

Directions

1. Wash and dry the berries. Slice any larger berries, such as strawberries, into bite-size pieces.
2. In a mixing bowl, beat the heavy cream (or Greek yogurt) until it forms soft peaks. If desired, add sugar to sweeten the cream.

3. Serve the berries in individual bowls or glasses, topped with a dollop of whipped cream or Greek yogurt.

Per Serving: Calories: 150 | Fat: 12g | Carbohydrates: 9g | Fiber: 2g | Protein: 2g

2. Baked apples with cinnamon and walnuts

Preparation time: 10 minutes

Cook time: 40 minutes

Servings: 4

Ingredients:

- 4 medium-sized apples (such as Granny Smith or Honeycrisp)
- 1/2 cup chopped walnuts
- 1/4 cup brown sugar
- 2 teaspoons ground cinnamon
- 2 tablespoons unsalted butter, melted

Directions

1. Preheat the oven to 375°F (190°C).
2. Wash and dry the apples. Use a sharp knife or apple corer to remove the cores and seeds from the center of each apple.
3. In a small bowl, mix together the chopped walnuts, brown sugar, and cinnamon.
4. Stuff each apple with the walnut mixture, pressing it down into the cavity.
5. Place the stuffed apples in a baking dish and drizzle them with the melted butter.
6. Bake for 40 minutes, or until the apples are tender and the filling is lightly browned.
7. Serve the baked apples warm, garnished with additional chopped walnuts and a sprinkle of cinnamon if desired.

Per Serving: Calories: 270 | Fat: 12g | Carbohydrates: 43g | Fiber: 6g | Protein: 3g

3. Sugar-free chocolate mousse

Preparation time: 10 minutes

Chill time: 2 hours

Servings: 4

Ingredients:

- 1/2 cup heavy whipping cream
- 1/2 cup unsweetened cocoa powder
- 1/2 cup plain Greek yogurt
- 1/4 cup powdered erythritol or another sugar substitute
- 1 teaspoon vanilla extract

Directions

1. In a mixing bowl, beat the heavy cream until it forms soft peaks.

2. In a separate mixing bowl, whisk together the cocoa powder, Greek yogurt, erythritol, and vanilla extract.
3. Gently fold the whipped cream into the chocolate mixture until well combined.
4. Spoon the mousse into individual dessert dishes or glasses.
5. Chill the mousse in the refrigerator for at least 2 hours before serving.

Per Serving: Calories: 140 | Fat: 12g | Carbohydrates: 9g | Fiber: 4g | Protein: 5g

4. Flourless chocolate cake with whipped cream

Preparation time: 15 minutes

Bake time: 25 minutes

Servings: 8

Ingredients:

- 1 cup semisweet chocolate chips
- 1/2 cup unsalted butter
- 3/4 cup granulated sugar
- 1/2 cup unsweetened cocoa powder
- 3 large eggs
- 1 teaspoon vanilla extract
- Whipped cream for serving (optional)

Directions

1. Preheat the oven to 375°F (190°C).
2. Grease an 8-inch (20 cm) round cake pan with cooking spray or butter.
3. In a large microwave-safe bowl, melt the chocolate chips and butter together in the microwave, stirring every 30 seconds until smooth.
4. Add the sugar, cocoa powder, eggs, and vanilla extract to the chocolate mixture and stir until well combined.

5. Pour the batter into the prepared cake pan and smooth the top with a spatula.
6. Bake the cake for 25 minutes, or until a toothpick inserted into the center comes out clean.
7. Let the cake cool in the pan for 5 minutes before transferring it to a wire rack to cool completely.
8. Serve slices of the cake with whipped cream if desired.

Per Serving: Calories: 350 | Fat: 23g | Carbohydrates: 35g | Fiber: 3g | Protein: 4g

5. Peanut butter and banana bites

Preparation time: 5 minutes

Servings: 2

Ingredients:

- 1 large banana
- 2 tablespoons peanut butter
- 2 tablespoons granola
- 1 tablespoon honey

Directions

1. Peel the banana and slice it into 1/2-inch (1 cm) rounds.
2. Spread peanut butter on one side of each banana slice.
3. Sprinkle granola over the peanut butter on each slice.
4. Drizzle honey over the granola on each slice.
5. Serve immediately or refrigerate until ready to eat.

Per Serving: | Calories: 220 | Fat: 9g | Carbohydrates: 33g | Fiber: 3g | Protein: 5g

6. Frozen Greek yogurt with mixed berries

Preparation time: 10 minutes

Freeze time: 4 hours

Servings: 4

Ingredients:

- 2 cups plain Greek yogurt
- 1 cup mixed berries (fresh or frozen)
- 1/4 cup honey or other liquid sweetener
- 1 teaspoon vanilla extract

Directions

1. In a blender or food processor, puree the berries until smooth.
2. Add the Greek yogurt, honey, and vanilla extract to the blender and blend again until well combined.
3. Pour the mixture into a freezer-safe container and cover with a lid or plastic wrap.
4. Freeze the yogurt for 4 hours or until it is firm.
5. When ready to serve, let the yogurt sit at room temperature for a few minutes to soften before scooping into bowls or glasses.

Per Serving: Calories: 140 | Fat: 0g | Carbohydrates: 26g | Fiber: 2g | Protein: 12g

7. Chia seed pudding with coconut milk

Preparation time: 5 minutes

Chill time: 4 hours or overnight

Servings: 2

Ingredients:

1/2 cup chia seeds

2 cups unsweetened coconut milk

1/4 cup honey or other liquid sweetener

1/2 teaspoon vanilla extract

Mixed berries for serving (optional)

Directions

1. In a large bowl, whisk together the chia seeds, coconut milk, honey, and vanilla extract until well combined.
2. Pour the mixture into a container with a lid or individual serving cups.
3. Cover the container or cups and refrigerate for at least 4 hours or overnight.
4. When ready to serve, top each serving with mixed berries if desired.

Per Serving: Calories: 330 | Fat: 18g | Carbohydrates: 35g | Fiber: 17g | Protein: 8g

8. Baked pears with cinnamon and walnuts

Preparation time: 10 minutes

Bake time: 30 minutes

Servings: 4

Ingredients:

- 4 ripe pears
- 2 tablespoons honey
- 1/2 teaspoon ground cinnamon
- 1/4 cup chopped walnuts

Directions

1. Preheat the oven to 375°F (190°C).
2. Cut the pears in half lengthwise and remove the cores with a spoon.
3. Arrange the pear halves cut-side up in a baking dish.
4. Drizzle honey over the pear halves and sprinkle with cinnamon.
5. Sprinkle chopped walnuts over the pears.
6. Bake for 30 minutes or until the pears are tender.
7. Serve warm or at room temperature.

Per Serving: Calories: 140 | Fat: 5g | Carbohydrates: 27g | Fiber: 4g | Protein: 2g

9. Coconut flour pancakes with mixed berries

Preparation time: 10 minutes

Cook time: 10 minutes

Servings: 4

Ingredients:

- 4 eggs
- 1/2 cup unsweetened coconut milk
- 1/2 cup coconut flour
- 1 tablespoon honey or other liquid sweetener
- 1/2 teaspoon baking powder
- 1/4 teaspoon salt
- Cooking spray or butter for greasing the pan
- Mixed berries for serving (optional)

Directions

1. In a large bowl, whisk together the eggs and coconut milk until well combined.
2. Add the coconut flour, honey, baking powder, and salt to the bowl and whisk again until smooth.

3. Heat a non-stick skillet or griddle over medium-high heat.
4. Grease the pan with cooking spray or butter.
5. Scoop 1/4 cup of the pancake batter onto the pan for each pancake.
6. Cook the pancakes for 2-3 minutes on each side or until they are golden brown.
7. Serve the pancakes with mixed berries if desired.

Per Serving: Calories: 200 | Fat: 11g | Carbohydrates: 17g | Fiber: 6g | Protein: 9g

10. Sugar-free chocolate truffles

Preparation time: 10 minutes

Chill time: 1 hour

Servings: 12

Ingredients:

- 1 cup unsweetened cocoa powder
- 1 cup coconut oil
- 1/4 cup honey or other liquid sweetener
- 1/4 teaspoon salt
- Unsweetened cocoa powder or shredded coconut for rolling

Directions

1. In a small saucepan, melt the coconut oil over low heat.
2. In a large bowl, whisk together the cocoa powder, honey, and salt.
3. Add the melted coconut oil to the bowl and stir until well combined.
4. Chill the mixture in the refrigerator for 1 hour or until firm.

5. Scoop the chilled mixture into 12 equal-sized balls.
6. Roll each ball in unsweetened cocoa powder or shredded coconut.
7. Store the truffles in an airtight container in the refrigerator.

Per Serving: Calories: 200 | Fat: 18g | Carbohydrates: 10g | Fiber: 6g | Protein: 3g

11. Berry crisp with almond flour topping

Preparation time: 15 minutes

Bake time: 30 minutes

Servings: 6

Ingredients:

- 4 cups mixed berries (fresh or frozen)
- 1/4 cup honey or other liquid sweetener
- 1/2 cup almond flour
- 1/4 cup rolled oats
- 1/4 cup chopped almonds
- 1/4 cup melted coconut oil
- 1/2 teaspoon ground cinnamon
- 1/4 teaspoon salt

Directions

1. Preheat the oven to 375°F (190°C).
2. In a large bowl, toss the mixed berries with the honey until well coated.
3. In a separate bowl, mix together the almond flour, rolled oats, chopped almonds, melted coconut oil, cinnamon, and salt until crumbly.
4. Pour the berry mixture into a 9-inch baking dish.
5. Sprinkle the almond flour mixture over the top of the berries.

6. Bake for 30 minutes or until the topping is golden brown and the berries are bubbling.
7. Serve warm.

Per Serving: Calories: 240 | Fat: 16g | Carbohydrates: 24g | Fiber: 5g | Protein: 4g

12. Chocolate avocado pudding

Preparation time: 10 minutes

Chill time: 1 hour

Servings: 4

Ingredients:

- 2 ripe avocados, peeled and pitted
- 1/2 cup unsweetened cocoa powder
- 1/2 cup unsweetened almond milk
- 1/4 cup honey or other liquid sweetener
- 1/2 teaspoon vanilla extract
- Pinch of salt
- Fresh berries for serving (optional)

Directions

1. In a blender or food processor, blend the avocados, cocoa powder, almond milk, honey, vanilla extract, and salt until smooth.
2. Chill the mixture in the refrigerator for 1 hour or until firm.
3. Serve the pudding with fresh berries if desired.

Per Serving: Calories: 220 | Fat: 16g | Carbohydrates: 25g | Fiber: 9g | Protein: 4g

13. Greek yogurt cheesecake with mixed berries

Preparation time: 15 minutes

Chill time: 4 hours or overnight

Servings: 8

Ingredients:

- 1 cup almond flour
- 1/4 cup coconut oil, melted
- 2 tablespoons honey or other liquid sweetener
- 1/4 teaspoon salt
- 1 cup plain Greek yogurt
- 8 oz cream cheese, softened
- 1/4 cup honey or other liquid sweetener
- 1 teaspoon vanilla extract
- 2 cups mixed berries for serving

Directions

1. Preheat the oven to 350°F (175°C).
2. In a large bowl, mix together the almond flour, melted coconut oil, honey, and salt until well combined.
3. Press the mixture into the bottom of a 9-inch springform pan.
4. Bake for 12-15 minutes or until lightly golden brown.
5. In a separate bowl, beat together the Greek yogurt, cream cheese, honey, and vanilla extract until smooth.
6. Pour the mixture over the cooled crust.
7. Chill the cheesecake in the refrigerator for 4 hours or overnight.
8. Before serving, top the cheesecake with mixed berries.

Per Serving: Calories: 310 | Fat: 25g | Carbohydrates: 19g | Fiber: 3g | Protein: 8g

14. Strawberry shortcake with almond flour biscuits

Preparation time: 20 minutes

Bake time: 15 minutes

Servings: 6

Ingredients:

2 cups almond flour

2 tablespoons coconut oil, melted

2 tablespoons honey or other liquid sweetener

1/2 teaspoon baking powder

1/4 teaspoon salt

1 egg

1 teaspoon vanilla extract

2 cups sliced strawberries

1 cup whipped cream or whipped coconut cream

Directions

1. Preheat the oven to 350°F (175°C).
2. In a large bowl, mix together the almond flour, melted coconut oil, honey, baking powder, and salt until well combined.
3. Add the egg and vanilla extract to the bowl and stir until a dough forms.
4. Divide the dough into 6 equal-sized balls and flatten each ball into a biscuit shape.
5. Place the biscuits on a baking sheet lined with parchment paper.
6. Bake for 15 minutes or until lightly golden brown.
7. In a separate bowl, mix together the sliced strawberries and whipped cream.
8. To serve, cut each biscuit in half and top with the strawberry whipped cream mixture.

Per Serving: Calories: 360 | Fat: 28g | Carbohydrates: 20g | Fiber: 4g | Protein: 9g

15. Almond butter cookies

Preparation time: 10 minutes

Bake time: 12-15 minutes

Servings: 12

Ingredients:

1 cup almond flour

1/2 cup almond butter

1/4 cup honey or other liquid sweetener

1 egg

1/2 teaspoon baking soda

1/4 teaspoon salt

Directions

1. Preheat the oven to 350°F (175°C).
2. In a large bowl, mix together the almond flour, almond butter, honey, egg, baking soda, and salt until well combined.
3. Roll the dough into 12 equal-sized balls and place them on a baking sheet lined with parchment paper.
4. Flatten each ball with the back of a fork to create a criss-cross pattern.
5. Bake for 12-15 minutes or until lightly golden brown.
6. Cool the cookies on the baking sheet for 5 minutes before transferring them to a wire rack to cool completely.

Per Serving: Calories: 150 | Fat: 11g | Carbohydrates: 9g | Fiber: 2g | Protein: 5g

16. Berries With Balsamic Glaze

A simple yet delicious brunch dish made with fresh berries drizzled with a sweet and tangy balsamic glaze.

Prep time: 5 minutes

Cook time: 10 minutes

Serving: 4 people

Yield: 4 servings

Ingredients:

- 2 cups of mixed berries (such as strawberries, raspberries, blackberries, and blueberries)
- 1/4 cup of balsamic vinegar
- 2 tbsp of honey
- 1 tsp of cornstarch
- 1 tsp of water

Method of preparation:

1. In a small saucepan, combine the balsamic vinegar and honey. Bring to a simmer over medium heat.
2. In a small bowl, mix the cornstarch and water together to create a slurry.
3. Slowly pour the slurry into the saucepan with the balsamic and honey mixture, stirring constantly.
4. Cook for an additional 2-3 minutes, or until the mixture thickens.
5. Remove from heat and let it cool for a few minutes.
6. Place the berries in a serving dish, and pour the balsamic glaze over the berries.
7. Serve and enjoy!

Nutritional facts (per serving): Calories: 70 | Fat: 0g | Protein: 1g | Carbohydrates: 18g | Fiber: 2g | Sugar: 14g

17. Blueberry Sorbet

A refreshing and healthy brunch dish made with fresh blueberries and a touch of honey, frozen and blended to create a delicious sorbet.

Prep time: 10 minutes

Cook time: 0 minutes

Serving: 4 people

Yield: 4 servings

Ingredients:

- 2 cups of fresh blueberries
- 1/4 cup of honey
- 1/4 cup of water
- squeeze of lemon juice

Method of preparation:

1. In a blender, combine the blueberries, honey, water, and lemon juice. Blend until smooth.
2. Pour the mixture into a loaf pan and freeze for at least 4 hours or until firm.
3. Scoop the sorbet into individual serving dishes and serve immediately.

Nutritional facts (per serving): Calories: 80 | Fat: 0g| Protein: 1g| Carbohydrates: 21g| Fiber: 2g| Sugar: 17g

18. Chocolate Avocado Mousse

A rich and creamy brunch dish made with ripe avocados, cocoa powder and honey, blended to create a delicious and healthy chocolate mousse.

Prep time: 10 minutes

Cook time: 0 minutes

Serving: 4 people

Yield: 4 servings

Ingredients:

2 ripe avocados

1/4 cup of cocoa powder

2 tbsp of honey

1 tsp of vanilla extract

pinch of salt

Method of preparation

8. Cut the avocados in half and remove the pit. Scoop out the flesh and place it in a food processor or blender.
9. Add the cocoa powder, honey, vanilla extract, and salt to the food processor.
10. Blend until smooth and creamy.
11. Taste and adjust sweetness and seasoning as needed.
12. Spoon the mousse into individual serving dishes and chill in the refrigerator for at least 30 minutes before serving.

Nutritional facts (per serving):

Calories: 150 | Fat: 12g | Protein: 2g | Carbohydrates: 12g | Fiber: 6g | Sugar: 7g

19. Coconut Milk Ice Cream

A creamy and delicious brunch dish made with coconut milk, honey and vanilla extract, frozen and blended to create a healthy and dairy-free ice cream.

Prep time: 10 minutes

Cook time: 0 minutes

Serving: 4 people

Yield: 4 servings

Ingredients:

1 can of full-fat coconut milk

1/4 cup of honey

1 tsp of vanilla extract

pinch of salt

Method of preparation:

1. In a medium mixing bowl, whisk together the coconut milk, honey, vanilla extract, and salt until well combined.
2. Pour the mixture into a loaf pan and freeze for at least 4 hours or until firm.
3. Scoop the ice cream into individual serving dishes and serve immediately.

Nutritional facts (per serving):

Calories: 200 | Fat: 18g | Protein: 1g| Carbohydrates: 14g| Fiber: 0g| Sugar: 12g

20. Dark Chocolate Bark With Nuts And Seeds

A healthy and delicious brunch dish made with dark chocolate, mixed nuts and seeds, and a touch of sea salt, for a satisfying and nutritious treat.

Prep time: 10 minutes

Cook time: 0 minutes

Serving: 4 people

Yield: 4 servings

Ingredients:

- 8 oz of dark chocolate
- 1/4 cup of mixed nuts (such as almonds, walnuts, and pistachios)
- 1/4 cup of mixed seeds (such as pumpkin, sunflower and sesame)
- pinch of sea salt

Method of preparation:

1. Line a baking sheet with parchment paper.
2. Melt the chocolate in a double boiler or in the microwave.
3. Spread the melted chocolate onto the prepared baking sheet.
4. Sprinkle the mixed nuts, mixed seeds and sea salt on top of the chocolate.
5. Chill in the refrigerator for at least 30 minutes until set.

6. Break the chocolate bark into pieces and enjoy!

Nutritional facts (per serving):

Calories: 260 | Fat: 22g | Protein: 4g | Carbohydrates: 16g | Fiber: 3g | Sugar: 12g

1. Apple slices with almond butter

Preparation time: 5 minutes

Cook time: 0 minutes

Servings: 2-3

Ingredients:

- 1 large apple
- 2-3 tablespoons almond butter

Directions

1. Wash the apple and slice it into thin wedges or pieces.
2. Arrange the apple slices on a plate or tray.
3. Spoon the almond butter into a small bowl and serve alongside the apple slices.

Per Serving: (based on 2 servings): Calories: 168 | Fat: 12.3 g | Protein: 3.6 g |

Carbohydrates: 15.5 g | Fiber: 3.6 g | Sugar: 10.9 g

2. Carrot sticks with hummus:

Preparation time: 10 minutes

Cook time: 0 minutes

Servings: 2-3

Ingredients:

4-5 medium-sized carrots

1/2 cup hummus

Directions

1. Wash and peel the carrots, then cut them into sticks.
2. Arrange the carrot sticks on a plate or tray.
3. Spoon the hummus into a small bowl and serve alongside the carrot sticks.

Per Serving: (based on 2 servings):
Calories: 104 | Fat: 5.1 g | Protein: 3.8 g |
Carbohydrates: | 12.1 g | Fiber: 4.4 g | Sugar:
4.5 g

3. Cucumber slices with tzatziki sauce:

Preparation time: 15 minutes

Cook time: 0 minutes

Servings: 2-3

Ingredients:

- 1 medium-sized cucumber
- 1/2 cup tzatziki sauce

Method of Preparation:

1. Wash the cucumber and slice it into thin rounds.
2. Arrange the cucumber slices on a plate or tray.
3. Spoon the tzatziki sauce into a small bowl and serve alongside the cucumber slices.

Per serving (based on 2 servings):
|Calories: 73 | Fat: 5.2 g | Protein: 2.8 g |
Carbohydrates: 4.7 g | Fiber: 0.6 g | Sugar:
3.0 g

4. Celery sticks with peanut butter

Preparation time: 5 minutes

Cook time: 0 minutes

Servings: 2-3

Ingredients:

- 4-5 medium-sized celery stalks
- 2-3 tablespoons peanut butter

Directions

1. Wash the celery stalks and cut them into sticks.
2. Arrange the celery sticks on a plate or tray.
3. Spoon the peanut butter into a small bowl and serve alongside the celery sticks.

Per serving (based on 2 servings):
Calories: 109 | Fat: 8.4 g | Protein: 4.1 g |
Carbohydrates: 5.2 g | Fiber: 2.1 g | Sugar:
2.7 g

5. Hard-boiled eggs

Preparation time: 5 minutes

Cook time: 10 minutes

Servings: 2-3

Ingredients:

- 2-3 large eggs
- Water for boiling

Directions

1. Place the eggs in a pot and add enough water to cover them by 1 inch.
2. Bring the water to a boil over high heat.
3. Once the water is boiling, turn off the heat and cover the pot.
4. Let the eggs sit in the hot water for 10-12 minutes.
5. Drain the hot water and run cold water over the eggs to cool them down.
6. Peel the eggs and serve.

Per serving (based on 2 servings):
Calories: 143 | Fat: 9.9 g | Protein: 12.6 g |
Carbohydrates: 0.6 g | Fiber: 0 g | Sugar: 0.6
g

6. Greek yogurt with berries:

Preparation time: 5 minutes

Cook time: 0 minutes

Servings: 1

Ingredients:

- 1/2 cup Greek yogurt
- 1/2 cup mixed berries (such as strawberries, blueberries, and raspberries)
- 1 tablespoon honey (optional)

Directions

1. Wash the berries and slice any large ones into smaller pieces.
2. Spoon the Greek yogurt into a small bowl.
3. Top with the berries and drizzle with honey, if desired.

Per serving: Calories: 125 | Fat: 0.6 g | Protein: 16 g | Carbohydrates: 20 g | Fiber: 3 g | Sugar: 16 g

7. Roasted chickpeas

Preparation time: 5 minutes

Cook time: 25 minutes

Servings: 2-3

Ingredients:

- 1 can chickpeas (15 ounces)
- 1 tablespoon olive oil
- 1 teaspoon smoked paprika
- 1/2 teaspoon garlic powder
- 1/2 teaspoon onion powder
- Salt and pepper, to taste

Directions

1. Preheat the oven to 400°F (200°C).
2. Rinse and drain the chickpeas, then pat them dry with a paper towel.
3. In a bowl, mix the chickpeas with olive oil, smoked paprika, garlic powder, onion powder, salt, and pepper.
4. Spread the chickpeas in a single layer on a baking sheet.
5. Roast for 25-30 minutes, or until crispy and golden brown.

Per serving (based on 2 servings):
Calories: 204 | Fat: 7.5 g | Protein: 8.8 g | Carbohydrates: 27.5 g | Fiber: 7.8 g | Sugar: 5.5 g |

8. Edamame:

Preparation time: 5 minutes

Cook time: 5-10 minutes

Servings: 2-3

Ingredients:

- 1 cup frozen edamame (in pods)
- Salt, to taste

Directions

1. Bring a pot of salted water to a boil.
2. Add the frozen edamame and cook for 5-10 minutes, or until tender.
3. Drain the edamame and rinse with cold water.

4. Serve with salt, if desired.

Per serving (based on 2 servings):
Calories: 94 | Fat: 3.8 g | Protein: 9.1 g | Carbohydrates: 8.5 g | Fiber: 4.7 g | Sugar: 2.2 g

9. Baby carrots with ranch dressing

Preparation time: 5 minutes

Cook time: 0 minutes

Servings: 2-3

Ingredients:

- 1 cup baby carrots
- 1/4 cup ranch dressing

Directions

1. Wash the baby carrots and pat them dry with a paper towel.
2. Arrange the carrots on a plate or tray.
3. Serve with ranch dressing for dipping.

Per serving (based on 2 servings):
Calories: 82 | Fat: 6.6 g | Protein: 1.1 g | Carbohydrates: 4.6 g | Fiber: 1.4 g | Sugar: 2.9 g

10. Cheese and whole-grain crackers

Preparation time: 5 minutes

Cook time: 0 minutes

Servings: 2-3

Ingredients:

- 1 ounce cheese (such as cheddar or Swiss), sliced or cubed
- 6-8 whole-grain crackers

Directions

Arrange the cheese and crackers on a plate or tray.

Per serving (based on 2 servings): |
Calories: 138 | Fat: 8.6 g | Protein: 7.2 g | Carbohydrates: 10.1 g | Fiber: 1.4 g | Sugar: 0.9 g

11. Turkey and cheese roll-ups:

Preparation time: 5 minutes

Cook time: 0 minutes

Servings: 2-3

Ingredients:

- 4 slices turkey breast
- 2 slices cheese (such as cheddar or Swiss)
- 1/2 cup baby spinach leaves

Directions

1. Lay the turkey slices flat on a cutting board.
2. Place a slice of cheese on top of each turkey slice.
3. Arrange the baby spinach leaves on top of the cheese.
4. Roll up each turkey slice tightly and slice into rounds.

Per serving (based on 2 servings): |
Calories: 157 | Fat: 6.8 g | Protein: 21 g | Carbohydrates: 1.4 g | Fiber: 0.4 g | Sugar: 0.8 g

12. Roasted nuts (almonds, cashews, walnuts, etc.)

Preparation time: 5 minutes

Cook time: 10-15 minutes

Servings: 2-3

Ingredients:

- 1 cup mixed nuts (such as almonds, cashews, and walnuts)
- 1/2 teaspoon olive oil
- Salt and pepper, to taste

Directions

1. Preheat the oven to 350°F (180°C).
2. In a bowl, mix the nuts with olive oil, salt, and pepper.
3. Spread the nuts in a single layer on a baking sheet.
4. Roast for 10-15 minutes, or until fragrant and lightly browned.

Per serving (based on 2 servings):
Calories: 214 | Fat: 18.2 g | Protein: 6.6 g | Carbohydrates: 7.5 g | Fiber: 3.6 g | Sugar: 1.8 g

13. Air-popped popcorn with cinnamon

Preparation time: 5 minutes

Cook time: 2-3 minutes

Servings: 2-3

Ingredients:

1/4 cup popcorn kernels

1 teaspoon cinnamon

1/2 teaspoon sugar (optional)

Directions

1. Place the popcorn kernels in a brown paper bag.
2. Fold the top of the bag over a few times to seal it.
3. Microwave the bag on high for 2-3 minutes, or until the popping slows down.
4. Pour the popcorn into a bowl.
5. Sprinkle with cinnamon and sugar, if desired.

Per serving (based on 2 servings):
Calories: 70 | Fat: 0.8 g | Protein: 2.6 g | Carbohydrates: 15.1 g | Fiber: 3.6 g | Sugar: 0.7 g

14. Apple slices with cheese

Preparation time: 5 minutes

Cook time: 0 minutes

Servings: 2-3

Ingredients:

- 1 apple, sliced
- 2 ounces cheese (such as cheddar or brie), sliced or cubed

Directions

Arrange the apple slices and cheese on a plate or tray.

Per serving (based on 2 servings):
Calories: 130 | Fat: 7.3 g | Protein: 7.5 g | Carbohydrates: 12.2 g | Fiber: 2.5 g | Sugar: 8.4 g

15. Turkey and avocado roll-ups

Preparation time: 5 minutes

Cook time: 0 minutes

Servings

Ingredients:

- 4 slices turkey breast
- 1/2 avocado, sliced
- 1/2 cup baby spinach leaves

Directions

1. Lay the turkey slices flat on a cutting board.
2. Place a few slices of avocado on top of each turkey slice.
3. Arrange the baby spinach leaves on top of the avocado.
4. Roll up each turkey slice tightly and slice into rounds.

Per serving (based on 2 servings):
Calories: 176 | Fat: 10.3 g | Protein: 17.8 g | Carbohydrates: 6.2 g | Fiber: 4.5 g | Sugar: 1.2 g

16. Apple Slices With Almond Butter

This is a simple and healthy snack that combines the sweetness of apple slices with the creamy texture of almond butter.

Prep Time: 5 minutes

Cook Time: None

Serving: 1

Yield: 1 serving

Ingredients:

- 1 apple, thinly sliced
- 2 tablespoons almond butter

Method of preparation:

1. Slice the apple into thin slices.
2. Spread the almond butter over the apple slices.
3. Serve and enjoy!

Nutritional facts (per serving): Calories: 250 | Fat: 18g| Sodium: 0mg | Carbohydrates: 25g | Fiber: 5g | Protein: 6g.

17. Berry Smoothie With Chia Seeds

This smoothie is a delicious and healthy way to start your day. The combination of berries and chia seeds provides a powerful boost of antioxidants and omega-3 fatty acids.

Prep Time: 5 minutes

Cook Time: None

Serving: 1

Yield: 1 serving

Ingredients:

- 1 cup frozen berries (strawberries, blueberries, raspberries)
- 1 banana
- 1/2 cup Greek yogurt
- 1/2 cup almond milk
- 1 tablespoon chia seeds

Method of preparation:

1. Add the berries, banana, Greek yogurt, and almond milk to a blender.
2. Blend until smooth.
3. Stir in the chia seeds.
4. Pour into a glass and enjoy!

Nutritional facts (per serving)

Calories: 250 | Fat: 8g | Sodium: 40mgCarbohydrates: 40g | Fiber: 10g | Protein: 12g

18. Carrots And Hummus

This is a simple and healthy snack that combines the crunch of carrots with the creaminess of hummus.

Prep Time: 5 minutes

Cook Time: None

Serving: 1

Yield: 1 serving

Ingredients:

- 2 carrots, peeled and cut into sticks
- 2 tablespoons hummus

Method of preparation:

1. Wash and cut the carrots into sticks.
2. Serve the hummus on a plate or bowl.
3. Dip the carrot sticks in the hummus.
4. Enjoy!

Nutritional facts (per serving):| Calories: 70 | Fat: 4g | Sodium: 80mg | Carbohydrates: 8gFiber: 2g | Protein: 2g

19. Cucumber Slices With Tzatziki Sauce

This is a refreshing and healthy snack that combines the crispness of cucumber slices with the tangy flavor of tzatziki sauce.

Prep Time: 10 minutes

Cook Time: None

Serving: 1

Yield: 1 serving

Ingredients:

- 1 cucumber, thinly sliced
- 1/4 cup tzatziki sauce

Method of preparation:

1. Slice the cucumber into thin slices.
2. Serve the tzatziki sauce on a plate or bowl.
3. Dip the cucumber slices in the tzatziki sauce.
4. Enjoy!

Nutritional facts (per serving):

Calories: 50 | Fat: 3g| Sodium: 110mg| Carbohydrates: 5g| Fiber: 1g| Protein: 2g

20. Deviled Eggs With Avocado

This is a healthy twist on a classic deviled egg recipe. The avocado adds a creamy texture and a boost of healthy fats.

Prep Time: 10 minutes

Cook Time: 10 minutes

Serving: 1

Yield: 2 deviled eggs

Ingredients:

- 2 eggs
- 1 avocado
- 1 teaspoon Dijon mustard
- 1 teaspoon mayonnaise
- Salt and pepper, to taste

Method of preparation:

1. Place the eggs in a saucepan and cover with water. Bring to a boil, then reduce the heat and simmer for 10 minutes.
2. Remove the eggs from the water and place in a bowl of ice water to cool.
3. Peel the eggs and slice them in half lengthwise.

4. Remove the yolks and place them in a separate bowl.
5. Mash the avocado and add it to the yolks along with the mustard, mayonnaise, salt, and pepper. Mix well.
6. Spoon the mixture into the egg whites.

7. Serve and enjoy!

Nutritional facts (per serving): Calories: 250 | Fat: 22g| Sodium: 130mg| Carbohydrates: 6g| Fiber: 3g| Protein: 8g

CONCLUSIONS

Living with type 2 diabetes means accepting the presence of a faithful "life partner" who must become a companion and not an enemy. For this purpose, it is very important to change some behaviors and bad habits, which are the modes that identify our lifestyle.

In practice, for most people It means including moments in their week dedicated to physical activity, albeit moderate, such as walking, cycling or attending gentle gymnastics courses, as well as practicing physical activity, even at a more intense level, or a real sport, if the patient's conditions and state of health allow it and after an adequate training.

Changing your lifestyle also means being more aware of your diet, choosing healthy foods and moderate usual portions. Let us not forget that the person with type 2 diabetes is often also overweight or obese, may be hypertensive and with an altered level of cholesterol and blood lipids, or other associated diseases, all conditions that predispose to a greater risk of cardiovascular disease.

Changing your lifestyle also means understanding the need to deal with diabetologists and experts who ask their patients to have laboratory tests, to undergo checks, to discuss the trend of the most relevant elements for diabetes control such as the blood sugar diary, regular control of blood pressure, lipids and monitoring of complications.

All these elements make it clear that it isn't at all simple and obvious to accept and embrace coexistence with a chronic condition such as diabetes and it is also important to work psychologically to undertake a healthy lifestyle based on one's health.

60 - DAYS MEAL PLAN

Day	Breakfast	Lunch	Dinner	Desserts
1	Omelette with Spinach and Mushrooms	Black bean and corn salad with lime dressing and whole-grain tortilla chips	Spinach and Strawberry Salad with Feta Cheese and Balsamic Vinaigrette	Fresh berries with whipped cream or Greek yogurt
2	Greek Yogurt with Mixed Berries and Nuts	Mediterranean lentil salad with feta cheese and whole-grain pita bread	Roasted Vegetable Salad with Mixed Greens and Goat Cheese	Baked apples with cinnamon and walnuts
3	Cinnamon Apple Oatmeal	Three-bean salad with red onion and vinaigrette dressing	Broccoli and Cauliflower Salad with Raisins and Sunflower Seeds	Sugar-free chocolate mousse
4	Scrambled Eggs with Diced Tomatoes and Green Onions	Chickpea and vegetable biryani with brown rice	Caprese Salad with Fresh Basil and Balsamic Glaze	Flourless chocolate cake with whipped cream
5	Avocado Toast with Poached Egg	Black bean and sweet potato enchiladas with whole-grain tortillas	Greek Salad with Cucumber, Tomato, and Feta Cheese	Peanut butter and banana bites
6	High-fiber Cereal with Unsweetened Almond Milk and Sliced Banana	Lentil and vegetable chili with quinoa	Arugula and Pear Salad with Walnuts and Blue Cheese	Frozen Greek yogurt with mixed berries
7	Tofu and Vegetable Stir-Fry	White bean and kale soup with whole-grain bread	Kale and Quinoa Salad with Roasted Sweet Potato and Chickpeas	Chia seed pudding with coconut milk
8	Whole-Grain	Chickpea and	Grilled Vegetable	Baked pears with

	Pancakes with Sugar-Free Syrup	vegetable tagine with couscous	Salad with Feta Cheese and Lemon Vinaigrette	cinnamon and walnuts
9	High-Fiber Cereal with Unsweetened Almond Milk and Sliced Banana	Mexican quinoa bowl with black beans, avocado, and salsa	Beet and Goat Cheese Salad with Mixed Greens and Honey Mustard Dressing	Coconut flour pancakes with mixed berries
10	Chia Seed Pudding with Almond Milk and Fresh Fruit	Red lentil and vegetable stew with barley	Edamame and Vegetable Salad with Sesame Ginger Dressing	Sugar-free chocolate truffles
11	Smoked Salmon and Cream Cheese on a Whole-Grain Bagel	Mushroom and lentil shepherd's pie with mashed sweet potato topping	Carrot and Raisin Salad with Greek Yogurt and Honey Dressing	Berry crisp with almond flour topping
12	Vegetable Frittata	Tuna and white bean salad with whole-grain crackers	Tomato and Cucumber Salad with Avocado and Lime Dressing	Chocolate avocado pudding
13	Low-Carb Breakfast Burrito with Scrambled Eggs, Cheese, and Salsa Wrapped in a Whole-Grain Tortilla	Chickpea and spinach curry with quinoa	Grilled Asparagus and Bell Pepper Salad with Balsamic Glaze	Greek yogurt cheesecake with mixed berries
14	Quinoa Breakfast Bowl with Nuts and Seeds	Black bean and vegetable stir-fry with brown rice	Broccoli and Kale Slaw with Almonds and Cranberries	Strawberry shortcake with almond flour biscuits
15	Cottage Cheese with Sliced Peaches and Cinnamon	Lentil soup with carrots and celery	Roasted Brussels Sprouts and Sweet Potato Salad with Maple Mustard Dressing	Almond butter cookies

16	Omelette with Spinach and Mushrooms	Grilled Chicken with Roasted Vegetables	Chicken and vegetable soup with quinoa	Almond butter cookies
17	Greek Yogurt with Mixed Berries and Nuts	Lentil and vegetable soup	Baked Salmon with Roasted Asparagus and Quinoa	Strawberry shortcake with almond flour biscuits
18	Cinnamon Apple Oatmeal	Beef Stir-Fry with Vegetables and Soba Noodles	Tomato and vegetable soup with chickpeas	Greek yogurt cheesecake with mixed berries
19	Scrambled Eggs with Diced Tomatoes and Green Onions	Creamy cauliflower soup	Turkey Chili with Kidney Beans and Quinoa	Chocolate avocado pudding
20	Avocado Toast with Poached Egg	Lemon Herb Roasted Chicken with Roasted Vegetables	Carrot and ginger soup	Berry crisp with almond flour topping
21	High-fiber Cereal with Unsweetened Almond Milk and Sliced Banana	Split pea soup with ham	Grilled Shrimp Skewers with Mixed Greens and Quinoa	Sugar-free chocolate truffles
22	Tofu and Vegetable Stir-Fry	Baked Chicken Breast with Steamed Broccoli		Coconut flour pancakes with mixed berries
23	Whole-Grain Pancakes with Sugar-Free Syrup	Mushroom and barley soup	Pork Tenderloin with Roasted Sweet Potato and Green Beans	Baked pears with cinnamon and walnuts
24	High-Fiber Cereal with Unsweetened Almond Milk and Sliced Banana	Beef and Vegetable Kebabs with Quinoa or Roasted Potatoes	Minestrone soup with vegetables and beans	Chia seed pudding with coconut milk
25	Chia Seed Pudding with Almond Milk and Fresh Fruit	Roasted butternut squash soup	Turkey and Vegetable Stir-Fry with Soba Noodles	Fresh berries with whipped cream or Greek yogurt

26	Smoked Salmon and Cream Cheese on a Whole-Grain Bagel	Roasted Pork Loin with Brussels Sprouts and Sweet Potato	Roasted Butternut Squash Soup	Baked apples with cinnamon and walnuts
27	Vegetable Frittata	Turkey and Vegetable Soup with Quinoa	Baked Salmon with Roasted Brussels Sprouts	Sugar-free chocolate mousse
28	Low-Carb Breakfast Burrito with Scrambled Eggs, Cheese, and Salsa Wrapped in a Whole-Grain Tortilla	Grilled Chicken and Vegetable Kabobs with Quinoa or Roasted Potatoes	Creamy Tomato Soup with Lentils	Flourless chocolate cake with whipped cream
29	Quinoa Breakfast Bowl with Nuts and Seeds	Broccoli and Cheese Soup	Ground Turkey and Vegetable Skillet with Quinoa or Roasted Potatoes	Peanut butter and banana bites
30	Cottage Cheese with Sliced Peaches and Cinnamon	Herb Roasted Beef with Roasted Root Vegetables	Creamy Vegetable Soup with White Beans	Frozen Greek yogurt with mixed berries
31	Omelette with Spinach and Mushrooms	Chicken and Vegetable Soup with Barley	Grilled Salmon with Roasted Asparagus and Quinoa	Fresh berries with whipped cream or Greek yogurt
32	Greek Yogurt with Mixed Berries and Nuts	Baked Tilapia with Roasted Brussels Sprouts	Pan-Seared Tuna with Steamed Green Beans	Baked apples with cinnamon and walnuts
33	Cinnamon Apple Oatmeal	Shrimp and Vegetable Stir-Fry with Soba Noodles	Grilled Shrimp Skewers with Mixed Greens and Quinoa	Sugar-free chocolate mousse
34	Scrambled Eggs with Diced Tomatoes and Green Onions	Lemon garlic chicken with roasted vegetables	Baked Cod with Roasted Root Vegetables	Flourless chocolate cake with whipped cream

35	Avocado Toast with Poached Egg	Grilled Salmon with Roasted Zucchini and Eggplant	Seared Scallops with Roasted Cauliflower	Peanut butter and banana bites
36	High-fiber Cereal with Unsweetened Almond Milk and Sliced Banana	Poached Salmon with Steamed Broccoli	Grilled Shrimp and Vegetable Kabobs with Quinoa or Roasted Potatoes	Frozen Greek yogurt with mixed berries
37	Tofu and Vegetable Stir-Fry	Pan-Seared Salmon with Roasted Carrots and Parsnips	Broiled Halibut with Roasted Brussels Sprouts and Sweet Potato	Chia seed pudding with coconut milk
38	Whole-Grain Pancakes with Sugar-Free Syrup	Shrimp and Vegetable Stir-Fry with Soba Noodles	Grilled Swordfish with Roasted Root Vegetables	Baked pears with cinnamon and walnuts
39	Cottage Cheese with Sliced Peaches and Cinnamon	Apple slices with almond butter	Black bean and corn salad with lime dressing and whole-grain tortilla chips	Fresh berries with whipped cream or Greek yogurt
40	Quinoa Breakfast Bowl with Nuts and Seeds	Broccoli and Cauliflower Salad with Raisins and Sunflower Seeds	Carrot sticks with hummus:	Baked apples with cinnamon and walnuts
41	Low-Carb Breakfast Burrito with Scrambled Eggs, Cheese, and Salsa Wrapped in a Whole-Grain Tortilla	Cucumber slices with tzatziki sauce:	Three-bean salad with red onion and vinaigrette dressing	Sugar-free chocolate mousse
42	Vegetable Frittata	Chickpea and vegetable biryani with brown rice	Hard-boiled eggs	Flourless chocolate cake with whipped cream
43	Smoked Salmon and Cream Cheese on a	Greek yogurt with berries	Black bean and sweet potato	Peanut butter and banana bites

	Whole-Grain Bagel		enchiladas with whole-grain tortillas	
44	Chia Seed Pudding with Almond Milk and Fresh Fruit	White bean and kale soup with whole-grain bread	Roasted chickpeas	Frozen Greek yogurt with mixed berries
45	High-Fiber Cereal with Unsweetened Almond Milk and Sliced Banana	Cheese and whole-grain crackers	Chickpea and vegetable tagine with couscous	Chia seed pudding with coconut milk
46	Whole-Grain Pancakes with Sugar-Free Syrup	Mexican quinoa bowl with black beans, avocado, and salsa	Turkey and cheese roll-ups	Baked pears with cinnamon and walnuts
47	Tofu and Vegetable Stir-Fry	Apple slices with cheese	Roasted nuts (almonds, cashews, walnuts, etc.)	Coconut flour pancakes with mixed berries
48	High-fiber Cereal with Unsweetened Almond Milk and Sliced Banana	Turkey and avocado roll-ups	Mushroom and lentil shepherd's pie with mashed sweet potato topping	Sugar-free chocolate truffles
49	Avocado Toast with Poached Egg	Grilled Chicken with Roasted Vegetables	Chicken and vegetable soup with quinoa	Berry crisp with almond flour topping
50	Scrambled Eggs with Diced Tomatoes and Green Onions	Lentil and vegetable soup	Baked Salmon with Roasted Asparagus and Quinoa	Chocolate avocado pudding
51	Cinnamon Apple Oatmeal	Beef Stir-Fry with Vegetables and Soba Noodles	Tomato and vegetable soup with chickpeas	Greek yogurt cheesecake with mixed berries
52	Greek Yogurt with Mixed Berries and	Creamy cauliflower soup	Turkey Chili with Kidney Beans and	Strawberry shortcake with

			Quinoa	almond flour biscuits
53	Omelette with Spinach and Mushrooms	Lemon Herb Roasted Chicken with Roasted Vegetables	Carrot and ginger soup	Almond butter cookies
54	Cottage Cheese with Sliced Peaches and Cinnamon	Split pea soup with ham	Grilled Shrimp Skewers with Mixed Greens and Quinoa	Coconut flour pancakes with mixed berries
55	Quinoa Breakfast Bowl with Nuts and Seeds	Baked Chicken Breast with Steamed Broccoli		Sugar-free chocolate truffles
56	Low-Carb Breakfast Burrito with Scrambled Eggs, Cheese, and Salsa Wrapped in a Whole-Grain Tortilla	Mushroom and barley soup	Pork Tenderloin with Roasted Sweet Potato and Green Beans	Sugar-free chocolate truffles
57	Vegetable Frittata	Beef and Vegetable Kebabs with Quinoa or Roasted Potatoes	Minestrone soup with vegetables and beans	Berry crisp with almond flour topping
58	Smoked Salmon and Cream Cheese on a Whole-Grain Bagel	Roasted butternut squash soup	Turkey and Vegetable Stir-Fry with Soba Noodles	Chocolate avocado pudding
59	Chia Seed Pudding with Almond Milk and Fresh Fruit	Roasted Pork Loin with Brussels Sprouts and Sweet Potato	Roasted Butternut Squash Soup	Greek yogurt cheesecake with mixed berries
60	High-Fiber Cereal with Unsweetened Almond Milk and Sliced Banana	Turkey and Vegetable Soup with Quinoa	Baked Salmon with Roasted Brussels Sprouts	Strawberry shortcake with almond flour biscuits

Kitchen Measurement Abbreviations (Standard and Metric)

Abbreviation	Measurement
tbsp	tablespoon
tsp	teaspoon
oz	ounce
fl. oz	fluid ounce
c	cup
qt	quart
pt	pint
gal	gallon
lb	pound
mL	milliliter
g	grams
kg	kilogram
l	liter

Dry Measurements Conversion Chart

Teaspoons	Tablespoons	Cups
3 tsp	1 tbsp	1/16 c
6 tsp	2 tbsp	1/8 c
12 tsp	4 tbsp	1/4 c
24 tsp	8 tbsp	1/2 c
36 tsp	12 tbsp	3/4 c
48 tsp	16 tbsp	1 c

Liquid Measurements Conversion Chart

Fluid Ounces	Cups	Pints	Quarts	Gallons
8 fl. oz	1 c	1/2 pt	1/4 qt	1/16 gal
16 fl. oz	2 c	1 pt	1/2 qt	1/8 gal
32 fl. oz	4 c	2 pt	1 qt	1/4 gal
64 fl. oz	8 c	4 pt	2 qt	1/2 gal

| 128 fl. oz | 16 c | 8 pt | 4 qt | 1 gal |

Butter Measurements Chart

Sticks	Cups	Tablespoons	Ounces	Grams
1/2 stick	1/4 c	4 tbsp	2 oz	57.5 g
1 stick	1/2 c	8 tbsp	4 oz	115 g
2 sticks	1 c	16 tbsp	8 oz	230 g

Oven Temperatures Conversion

(Degrees) Celsius	(Degrees) Fahrenheit
120 C	250 F
160 C	320 F
180 C	350 F
205 C	400 F
220 C	425 F

Weight Equivalents US Standard Metric (approximate)

½ ounce	15 g
1 ounce	30 g
2 ounces	60 g
4 ounces	115 g
8 ounces	225 g
12 ounces	340 g

SCAN ME!

Printed in Great Britain
by Amazon

41116085R00064